"The Club"

Was all I needed to say when asked "what are you doing tonight" during my half mispent mid eighty's. Hey, I had a day job, and raced motorcycles during the summer months.

It was about the music, live energy in a tiny little place and fun people. Some weeks I'd stop in 5-6 nights to hear the band, see familiar faces. And it was eclectic, one of my favorite bands was the Wild Woody's, rock-a-billy was in with the Stray Cats on the charts and besides there was a certain sweetheart who would dance with me every time they played Pink Cadillac. Reggae at The Club, wonder if that influencd me to Jamaica for vacation rather than Los Angeles? Situated half way between Detroit and Chicago we had Motown sound as well as the Blues. From L.A. came Fishbone and Black Flag this could go on and on.

During the summer of 1986 I went down to The Club for a few nights with a camera, a pile of model releases, a tape rccorder and the idea for this book I didn't go inside, I hung out in front shooting and talking to people. The book was put together in 1987. One hard bound copy with prints as a layout and a seperate binder of the type. It was subsequently rejected by publishers. It was an expensive proposition pre-personal computers.

Twenty seven and a half years later! Here you go, for a very niche audience I'm sure. Those who where around The Club Soda in the mid eighty's. I hope you find yourself in this book, or see your friends with fond memories.

The qoutes are mixed, very, very few (but obvious) go with the photo opposite. It's certainly not a straight through read, flip it open, enjoy a shot and get a little kick out of the quotes. Take it light, we did back when.

One of my favorites is " someday when I'm like forty-five I can look at this book and say.....".

Well we're 50 now! and still rockin!

Copyright 1987 Randall J. Bohl

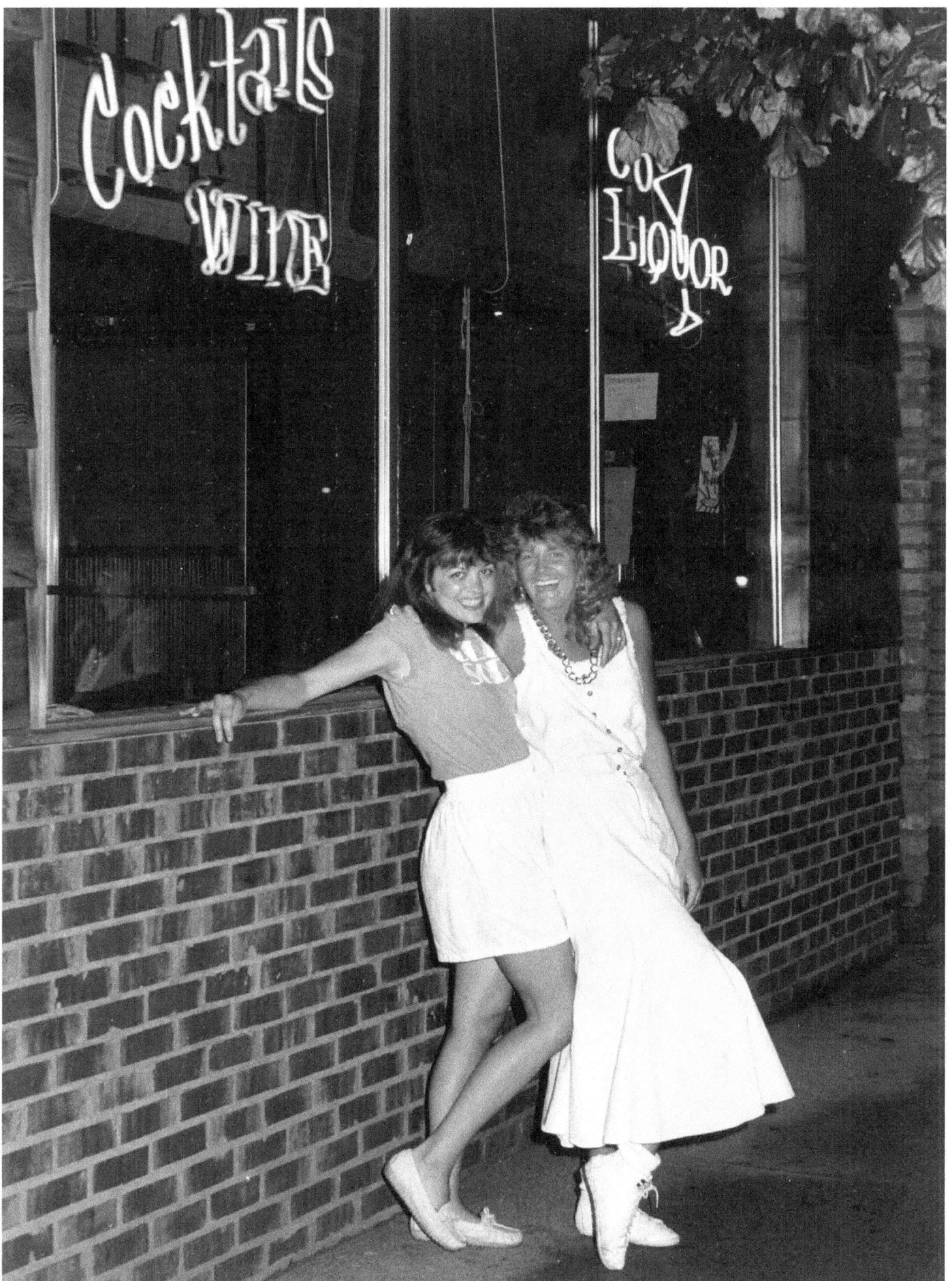

How can you say Arbis is "alright"? My favorite is of the kid in central park. That little boy in central park where he's going like this!

Are you a Warhol fan? youv'e gotta be.

I could do my Marilyn Monroe for you!

Hey this could be fun!

Carter, as in Jimmy, no relation.

It's a boring life but somebody's gotta live it.

Sexual persuassion, you gotta use it! If you've got it you might as well flaunt it, yep.

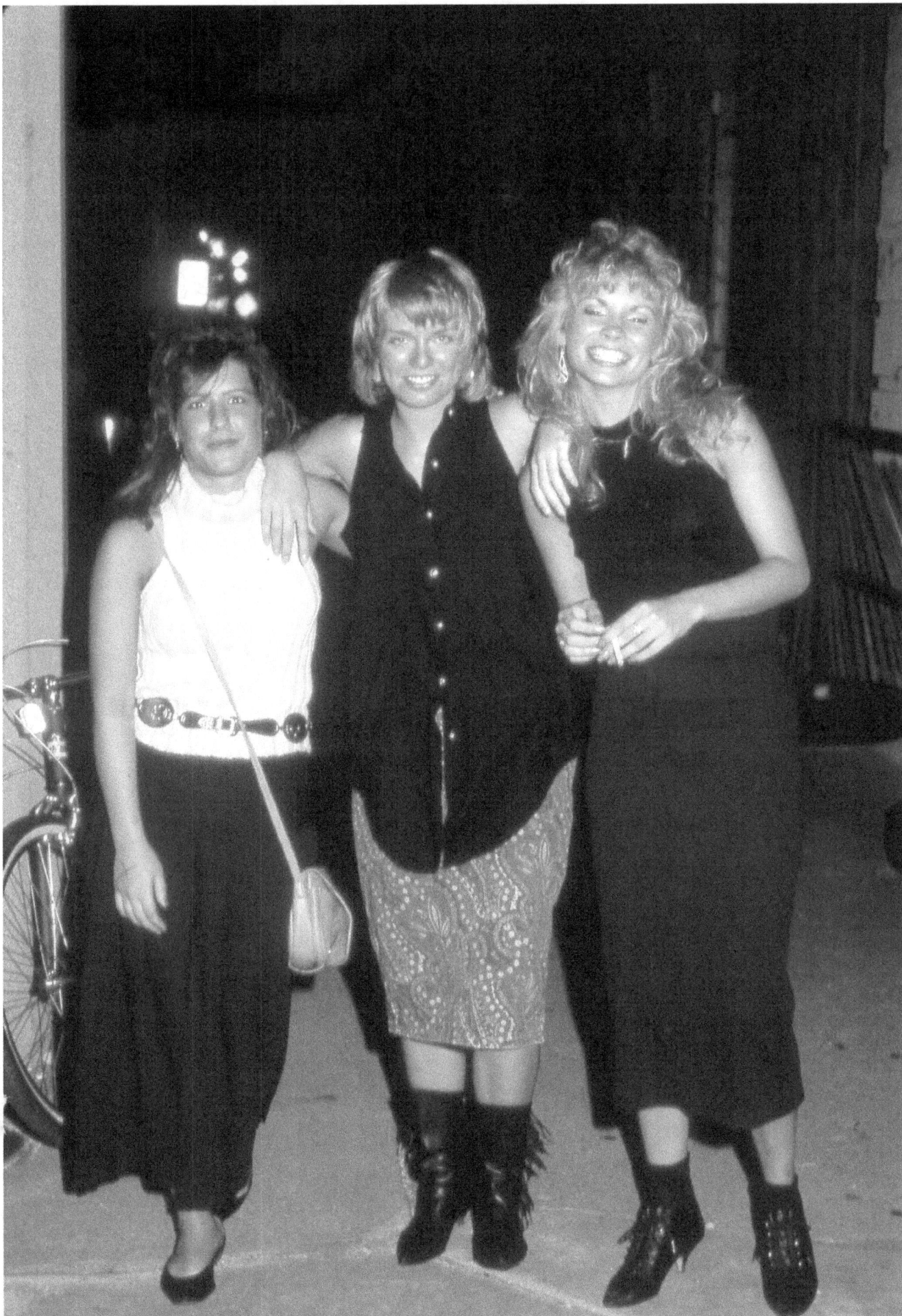

Oh god I hate it, I hate it there. The supervisors, their all assholes right now. Just can't win. I was doing next day air for a while, for a couple of weeks or for a couple of months rather. I was taking care of all the next day air. It was intense for a while and then they decided that they were canceling my position. They didn't need as many people so they moved me back to the unload. I hate it, basically stuff just like that. Now I'm just getting dirty and sweaty like the rest of them do. It sucks!

I'd have to get a little lower, or you a little higher.

You know what your going to have to do with this woman? You can't set it up because then she'll keep saying "I'm busy". Just say ok get your ass over here right now it'll only take ten minutes, you know "get over here now". I'm serious because if you try to plan something she's gonna go oh I'm busy I've got to go to the studio I've gotta do this I've gotta... Because right now she's working at the plant because their on stike and she's working like double shifts. This whole week she's gonna be double shifting from like eight to eight.
So you can catch her at nine you know.

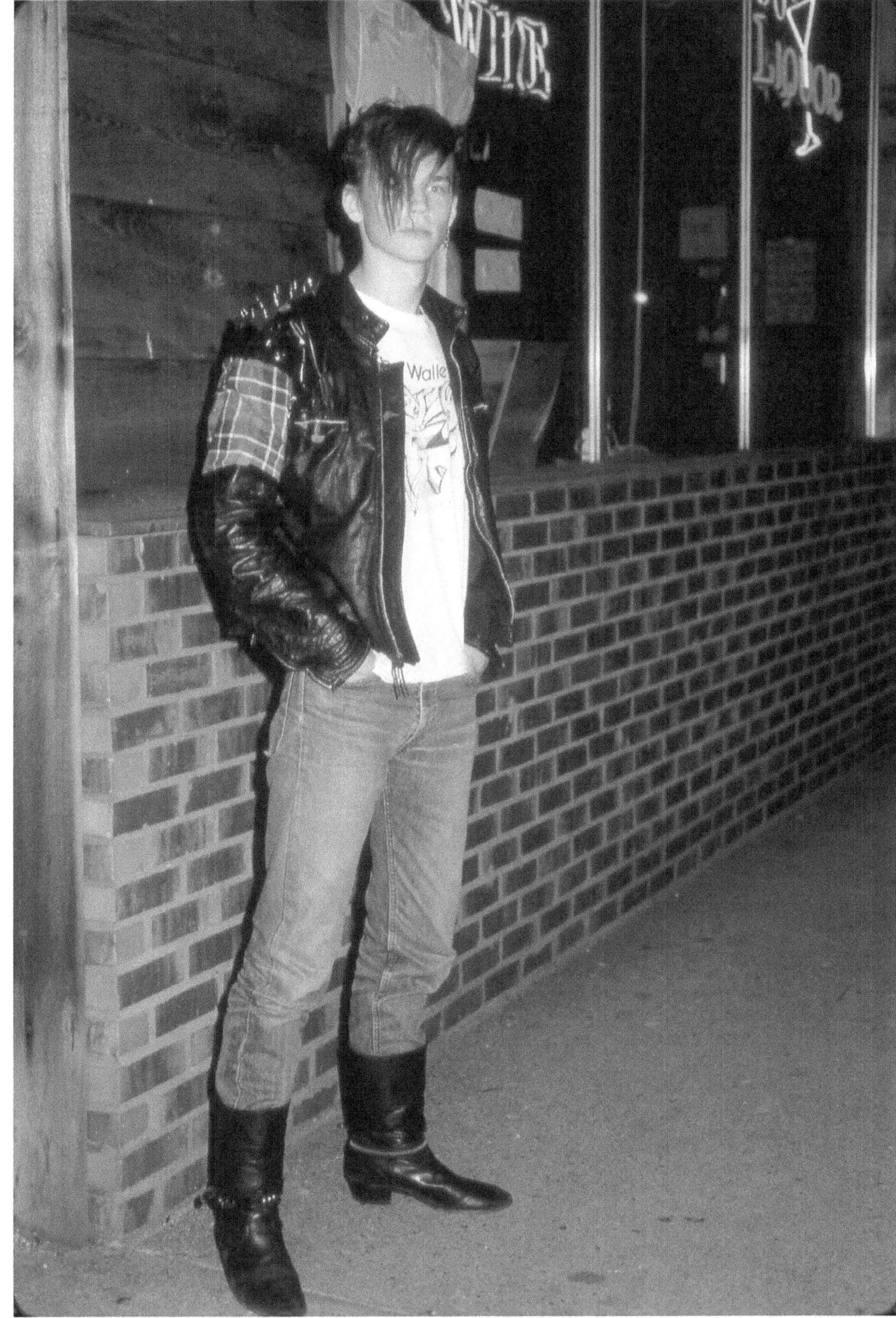

Im gonna give you my address so you can like-send me stuff.

You want us down in this asbestos stuff?

...because I'm working on my portfolio right now but all I have now is naked shit and I wouldn't mind some with clothes on.

I signed my life away when I worked at Cedar Point so....

Did you see them? Jesus and Mary Chain? It's just like something they put together to sell records you know.

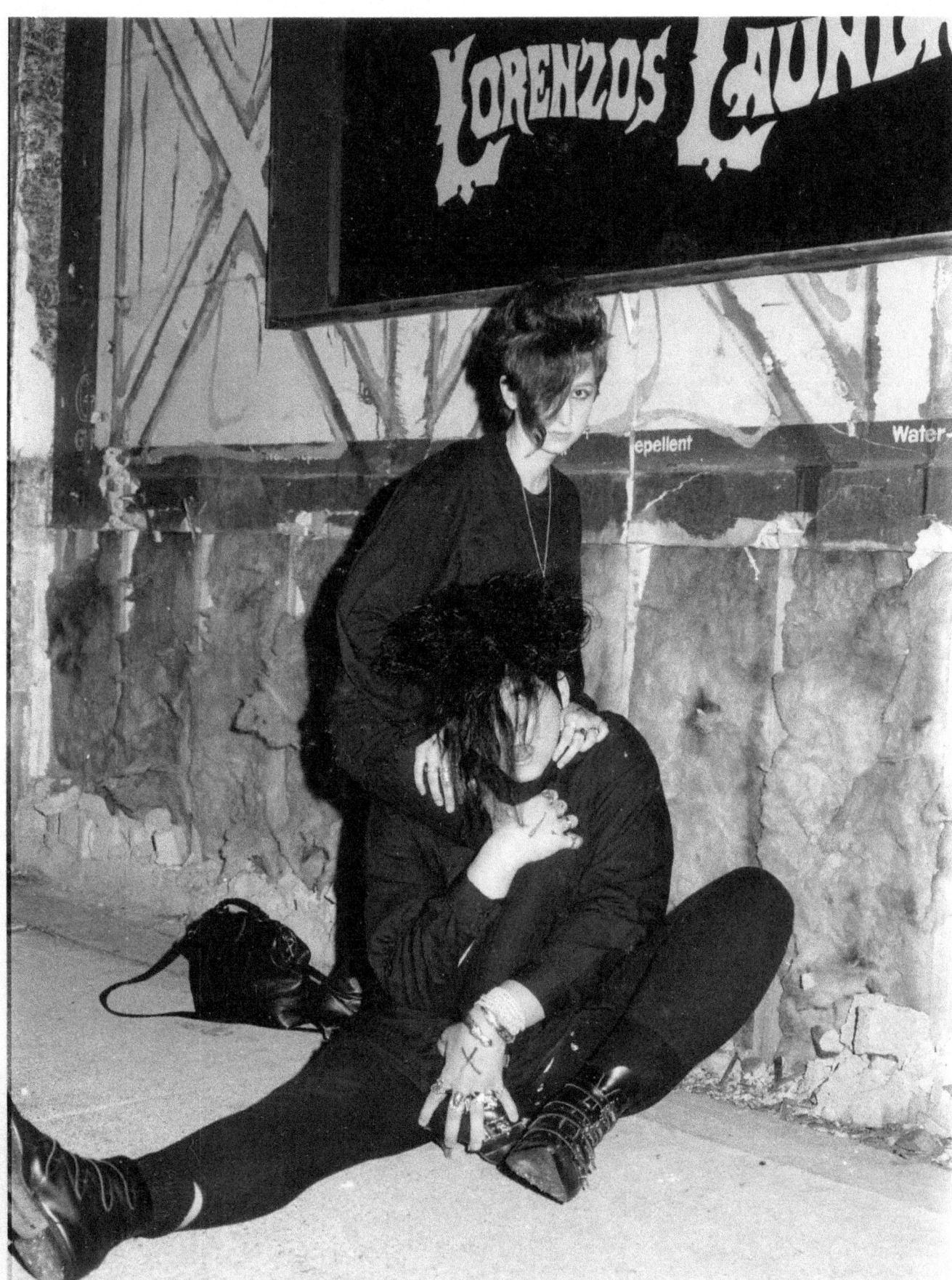

Someday when I'm like forty-five I can look at this book and say "jesus that was me?"

(on the Circle Jerks coming to town)
Hey who's putting up the three cases of beer for them? Yeah and the ten clean towels and the freshly squeezed orange juice.

Well gee you should head up to the Leland Hotel on Saturday night at about two or four, about that time you meet some really interesting people. Either that or Todds on a Thursday night, you'd get some good photographs there.

I was sitting on this ledge with a friend at this club and it was at night you know. I heard a gunshot and I go "wow that sounded real close". Then we heard two more gun shots and me and my friend go "wow lets move". So we like go out to the front of the building. There's a guy here, there's a guy here, here's the door, here's are car, here's the gunfire... it like freaked me out.

I'm cruising on a motor cycle with a friend of mine. We're like right at an intersection and this car pulls up in front of us, this guy sticks out his hand. He's got a gun in his hand, blows away a guy on a steet corner right next to us.
I just see this guy... gee that was fun.

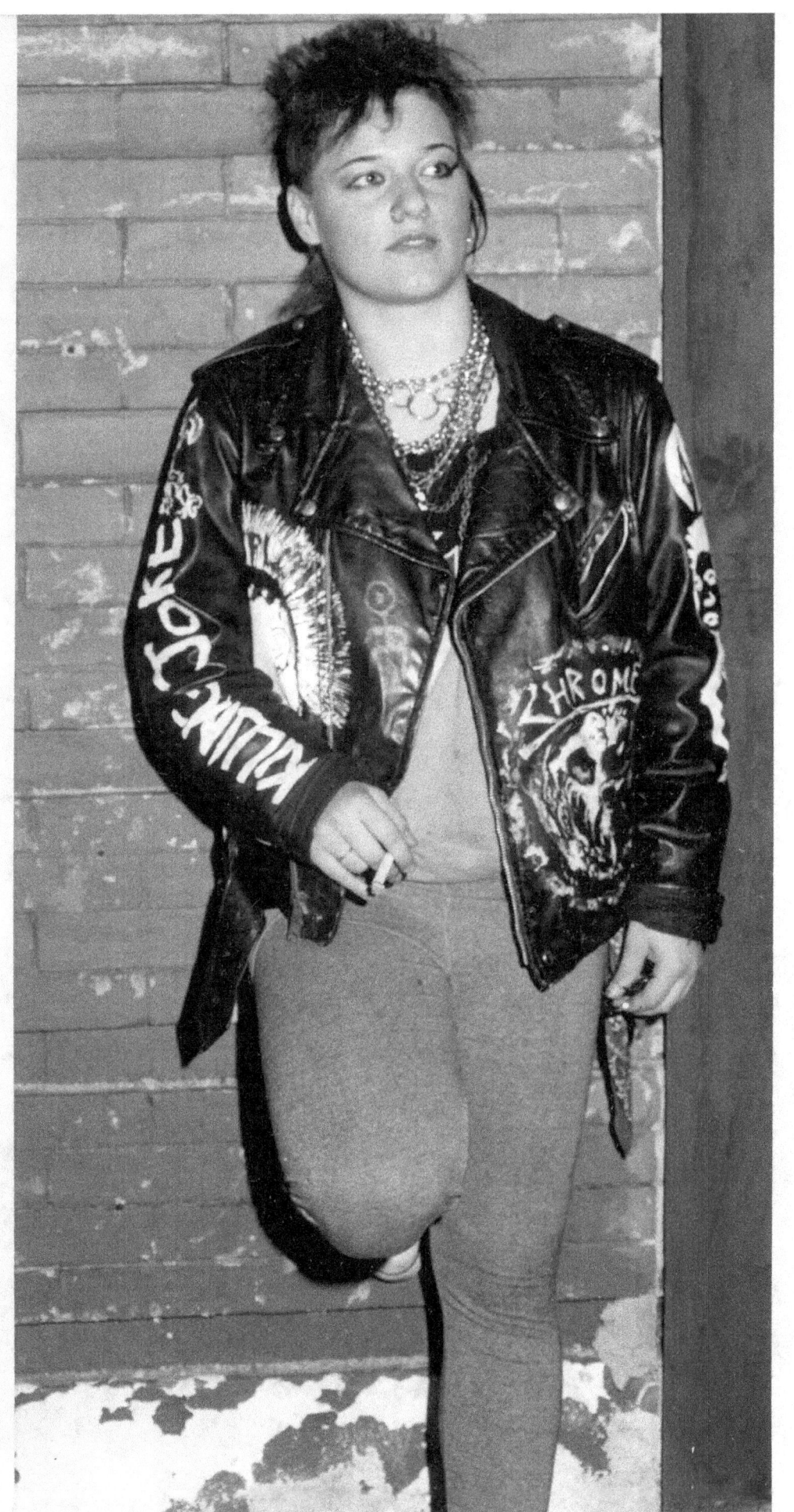

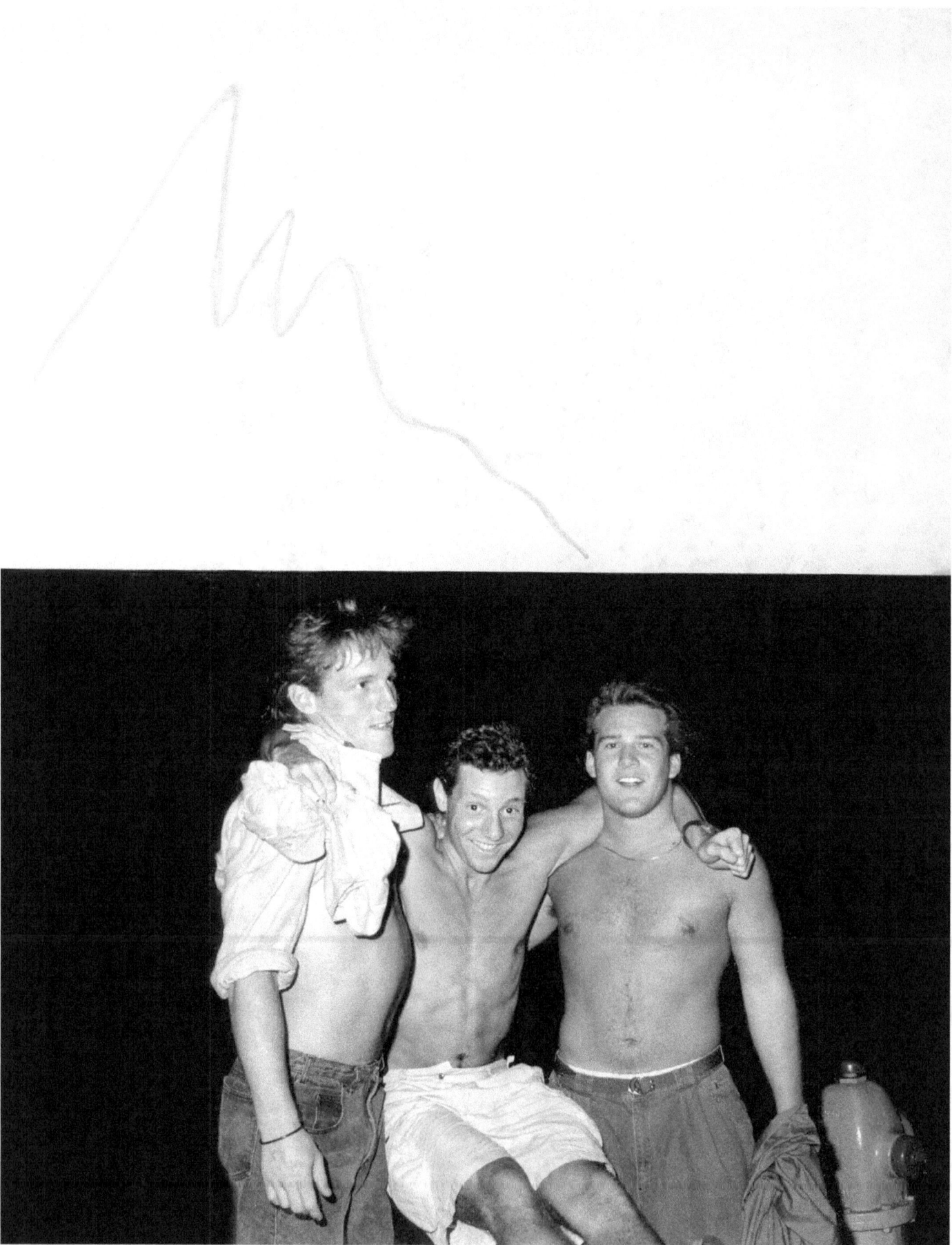

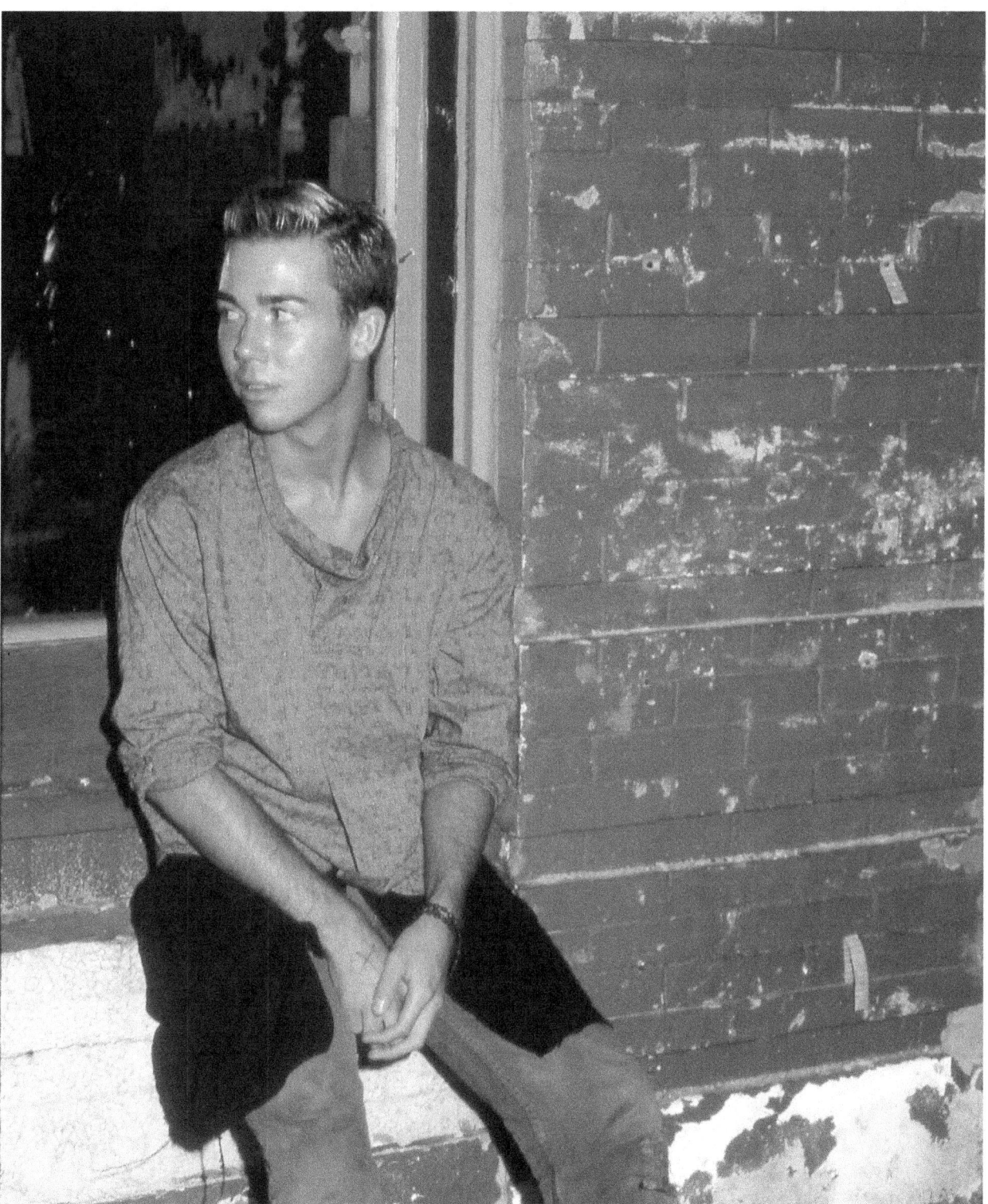

I don't know what I'm looking like. I haven't looked at myself in a while.

Want me to hang on the wall?
Want anything in particular?

I hate when I look drunk in photo's though. I mean they come out looking weird. You know when you just have to many and, we were just in Chicago. Just the other day this last week and we jumped in one of those little booths and took pictures you know how your basically when your eye's start rolling.

I was just hanging out looking for you, you know.

Oh my god I just saw the Richard Avadon show in Chicago. It's going to be there until the third. If you go to Chicago next weekend it'll be the last week it's there. God I don't know maybe it'll go somewhere else cool. Maybe it'll go to Detroit or somewhere like that.
It hasn't been to Detroit yet has it?

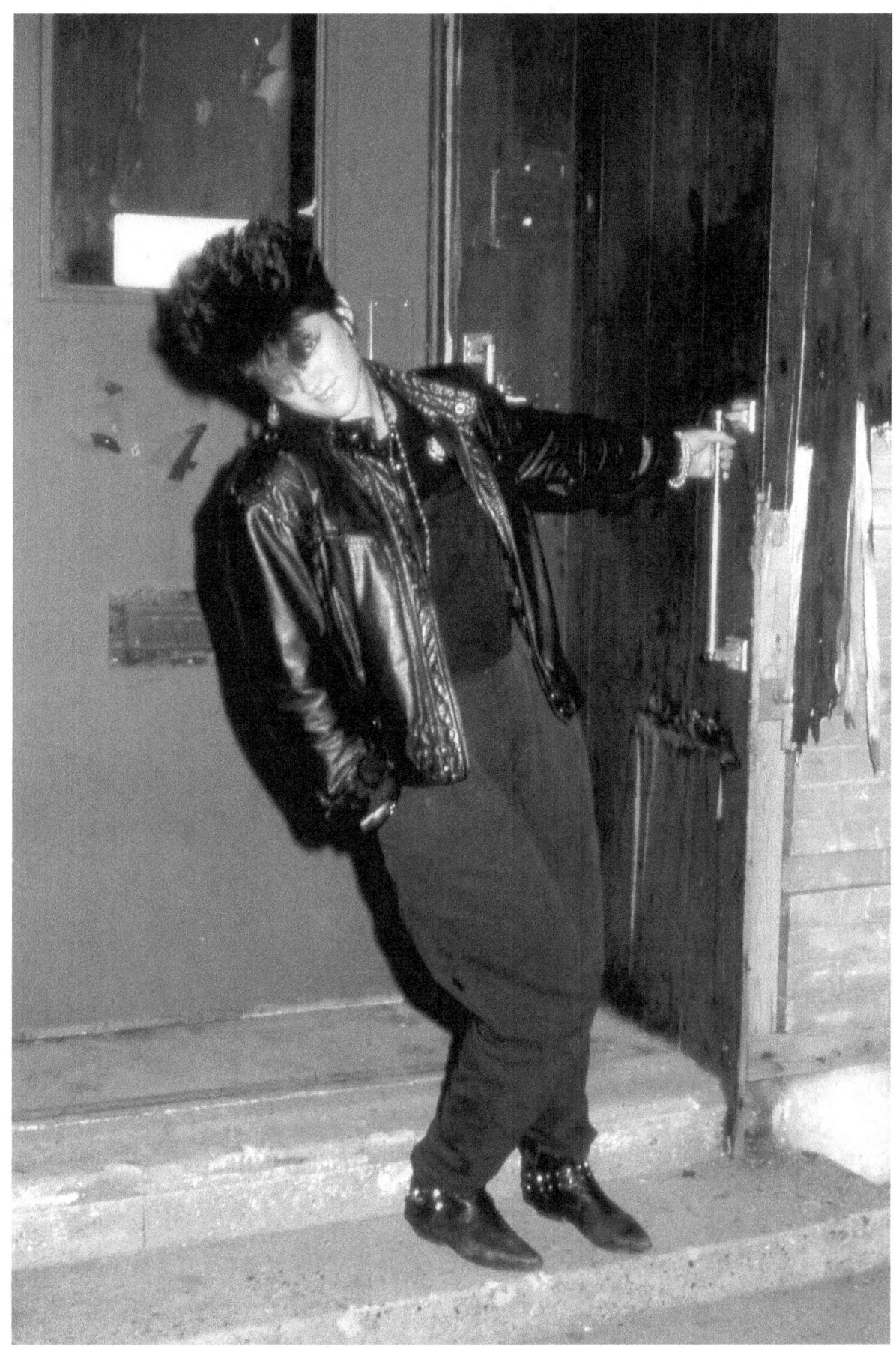

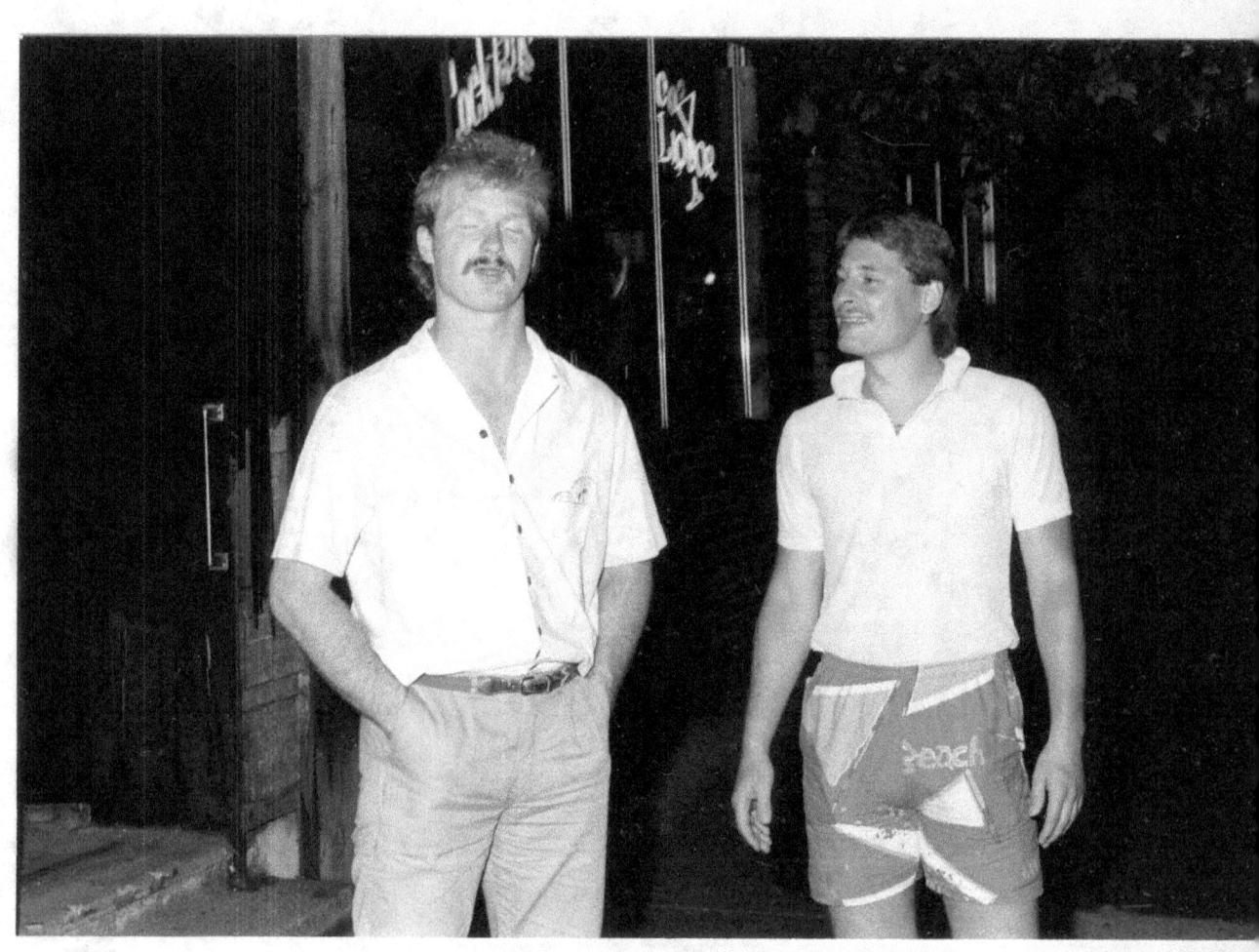

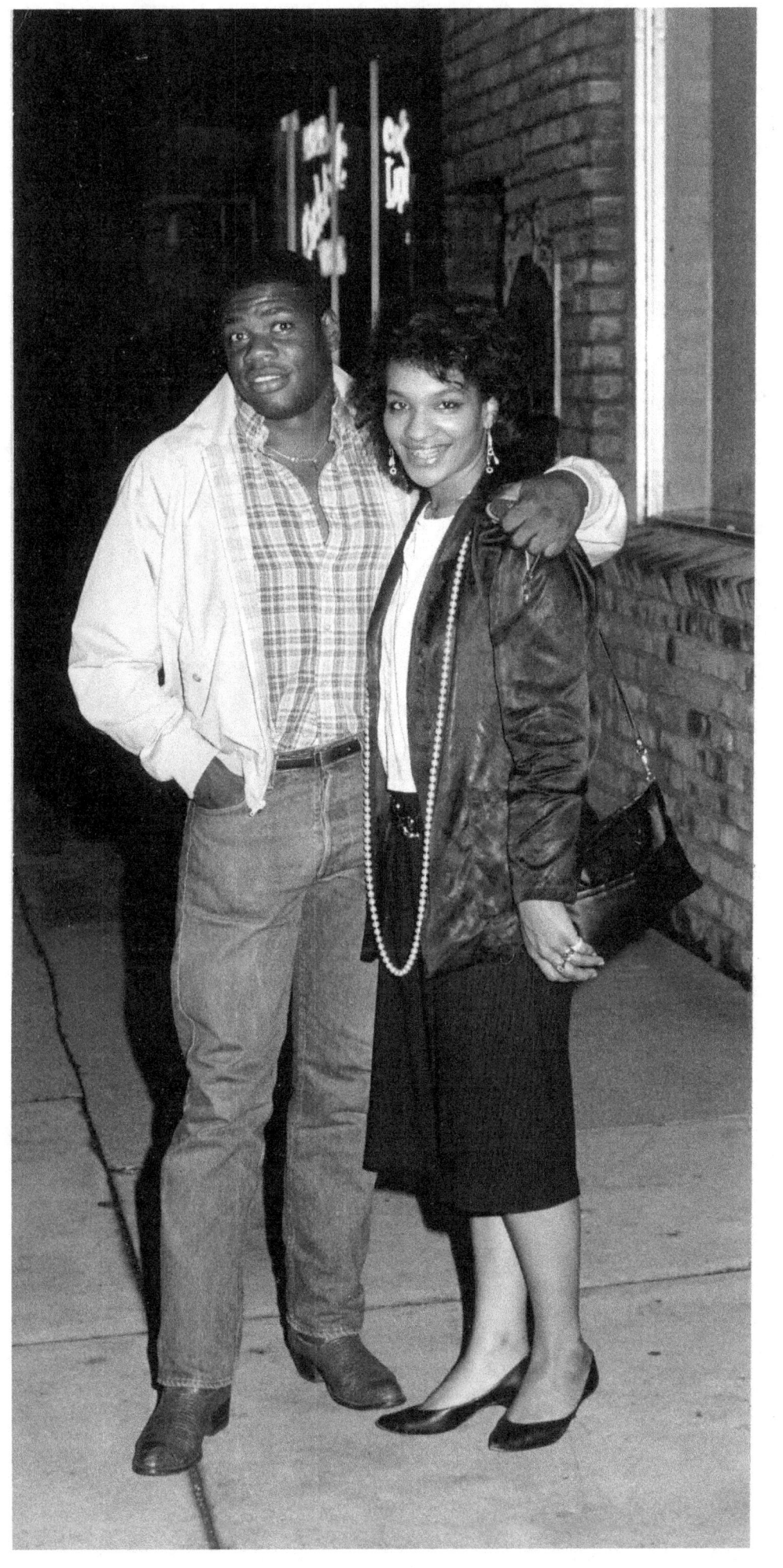

We're into reggae mon, we're from Kingston.
This guy's from Russia, you know Kingston mon?
Your signing your life away mon, says your in
the army- Siberia

I want to beat you up, but I can't afford it.

You don't know if their signing a different name?
"you can be Ali if you want"
resp: "but your white"

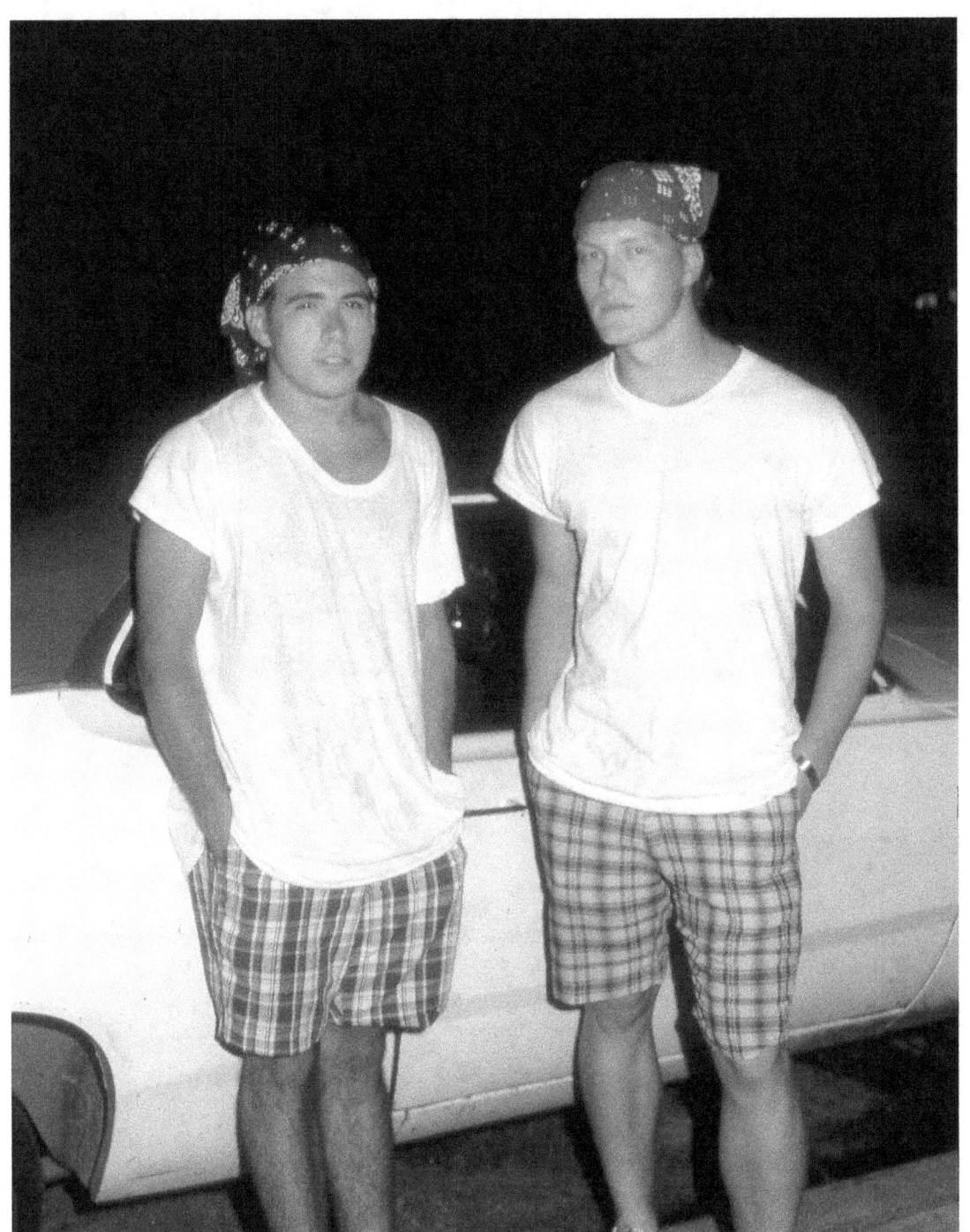

I'm just waiting to sign your book is it color or black and white? With this lady here? I've got five children. You want to see my drivers license? My pilots license? I don't know who you are, are you dutch? My great grandmother came from Austria do you know where Austria is?

Is she going to appear with me? My fathers 93 and he'll give me hell for walking this late at night. No that's not a very good background. I better turn my back, I didn't bring my sunglasses.

I don't like redheads.

What do you want me to do? lay down?

I want to find a thirty-nine year old virgin. I know where there's a lot of them, Nazereth College.

What have I got in here? Anything you want, fishing tackle, I got a lot of fishing gear and I got fishing bait.

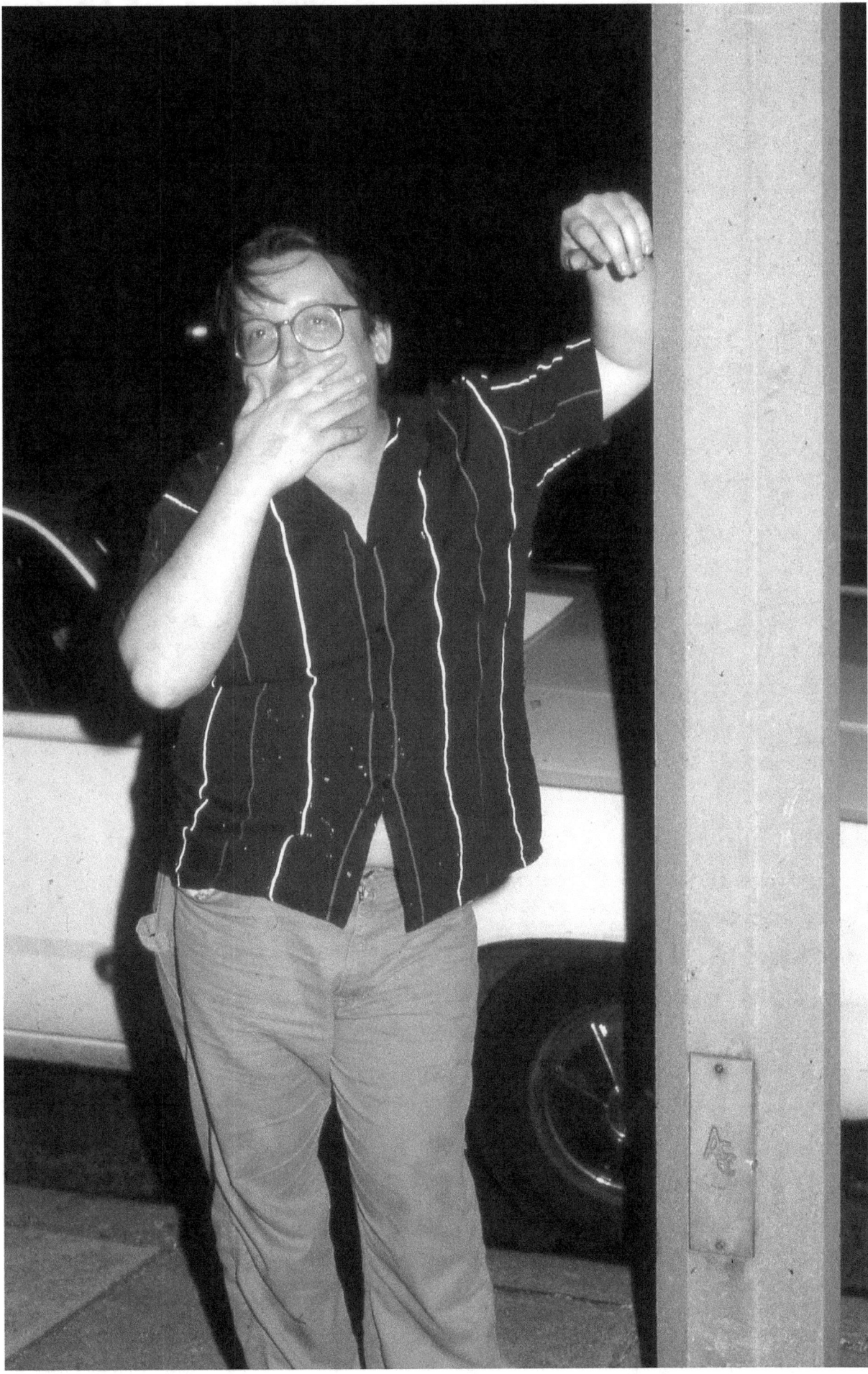

I used to live with a photographer, he moved away last fall. He had like the junkiest equipment but he took like the coolest pictures.

I had some sweet pictures too. I had just a bunch. I took a roll of black & white film of um... this close up of flowers & shit & the film got exposed.

What he used to do, what he used to do is go out at night and it was really cool because you know, he could do it. He could make it work.

You know who's also very good..... he put his film on the open thing, used it for exposure and this guy took sparklers and they made a big X time lapse. The whole background it was totally dark! and all you could see is the X.

Yeah there's this one picture he took of us that he took with.... we went to.... and we we're like drunk on tequila & shit. She and I and you know, what's his name? We walked back to the house. Like it was about this time of night, it was a full moon and he just like started to take pictures of us. There's one picture of us out on this wheel, it was like you know plastic with flowers and stuff all around it and it's night. Like I'm standing on top and she's holding a bouquet of flowers that we pulled. You know, where flowers come from.

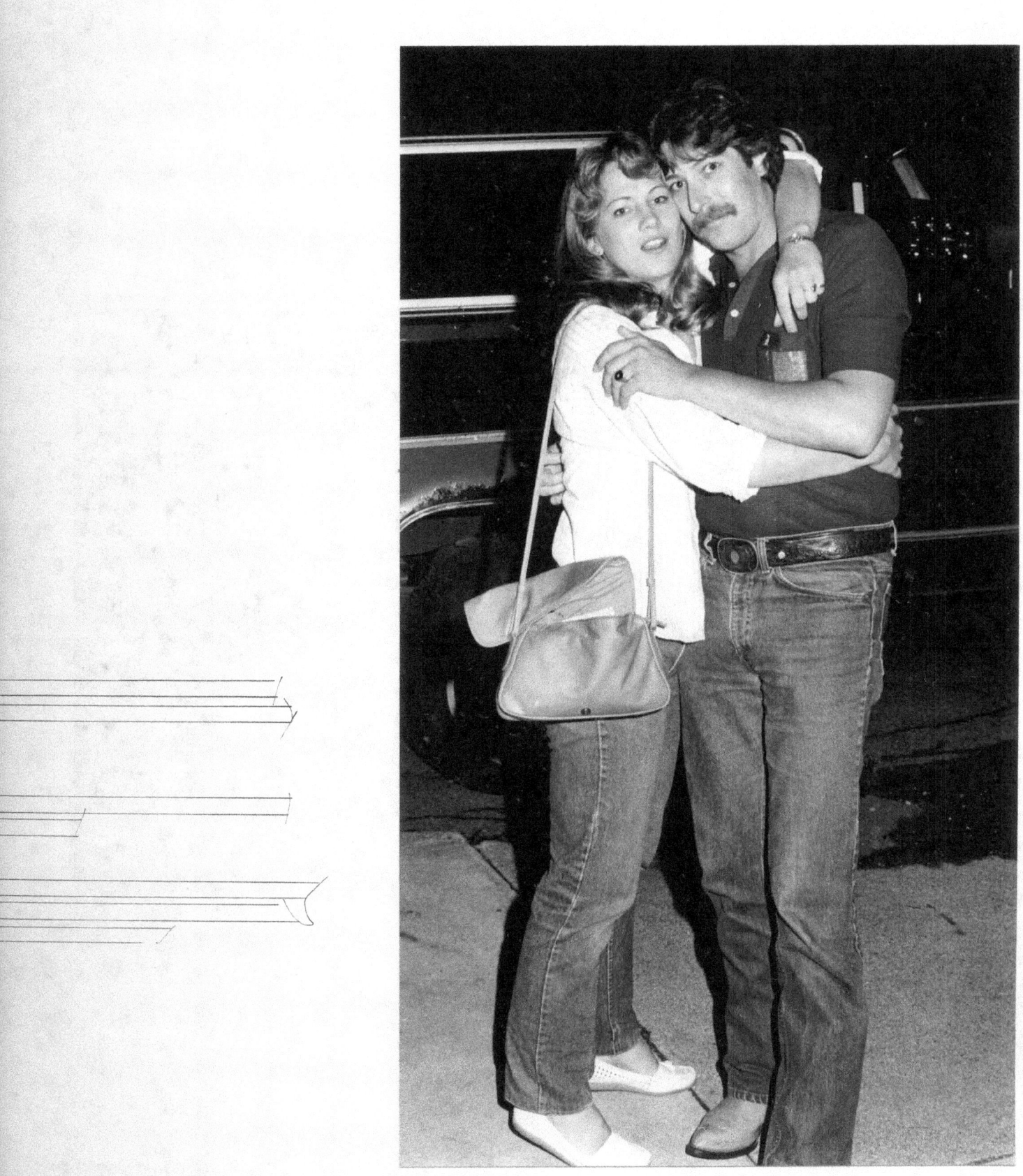

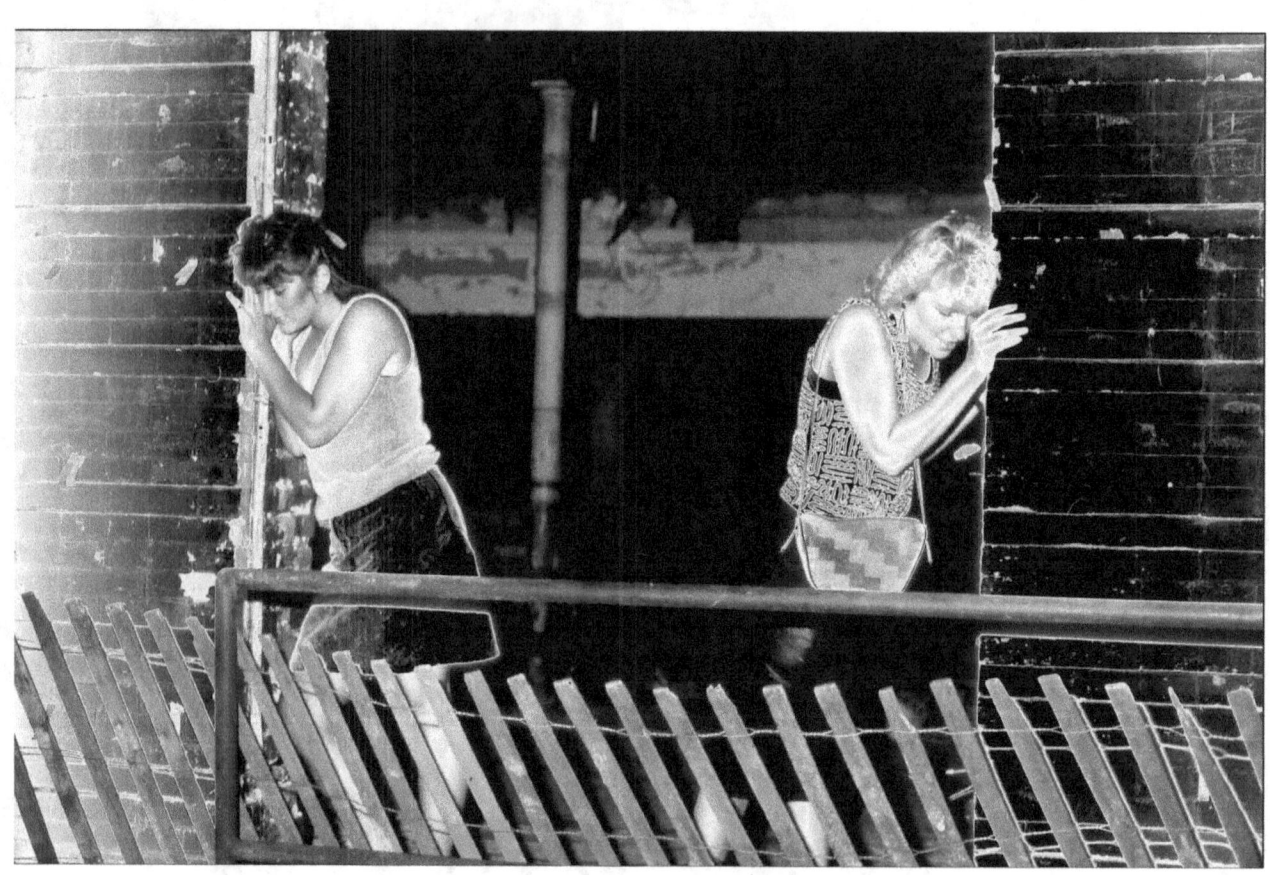

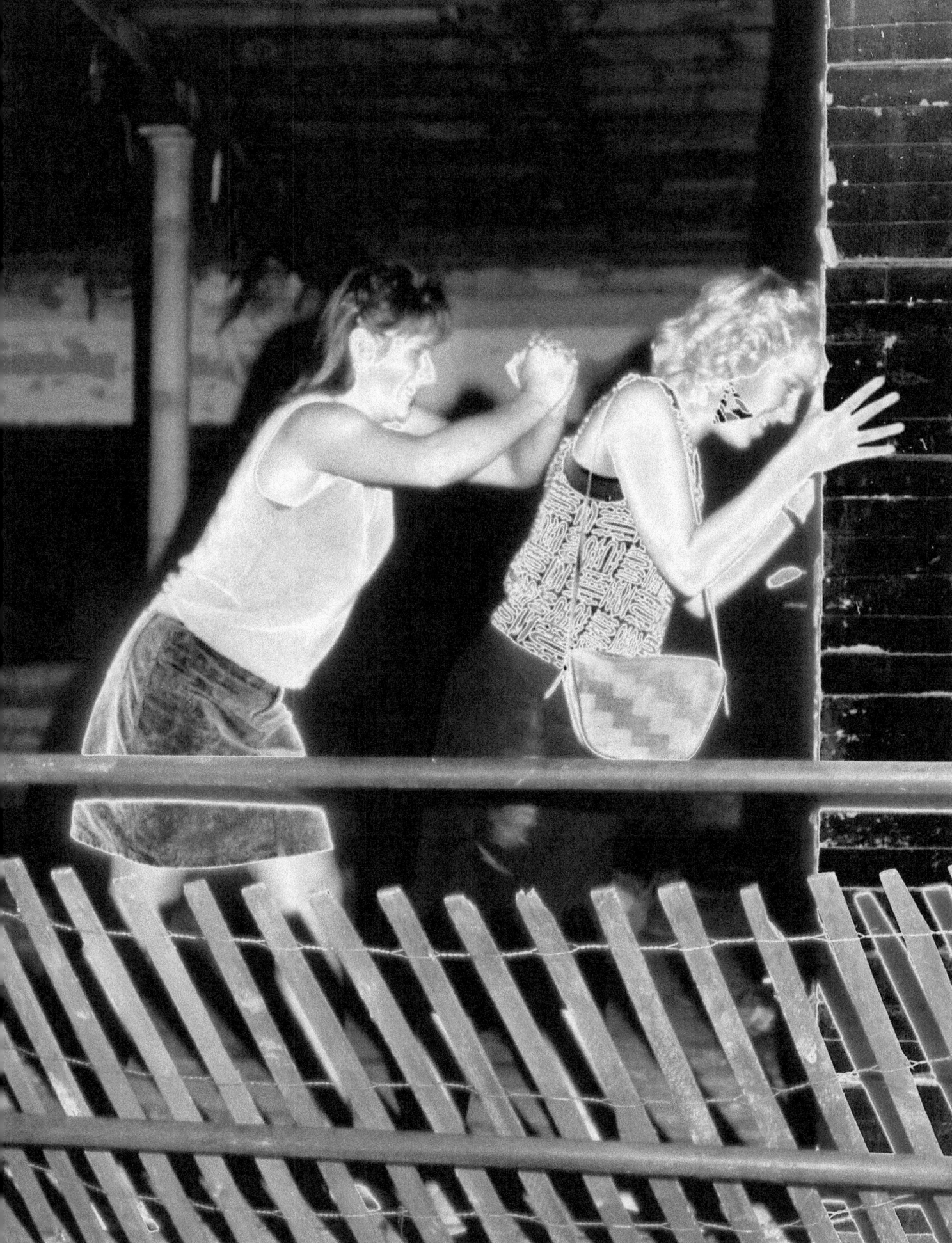

He took a picture of me in my bedroom once.
That one, that's up at our house.

Oh you took my picture once, is that okay?

That's fun I like that. Everybody likes getting their picture taken. I like to take pictures too.

Did she put her phone number down on this?

Wait has she been in these pictures yet?

I've been waiting to smash a Pinto. Let's get your car and give this guy something to take a picture of.
resp: " No lets get your car"

Hey this is us man!
This is the nightlife of Kalamazoo.

I have no pockets in the bottom of my pants.
It's like,
I have to grab my testicles when this happens.

It's good to see art happening in Kalamazoo.

Where do you want to go next?

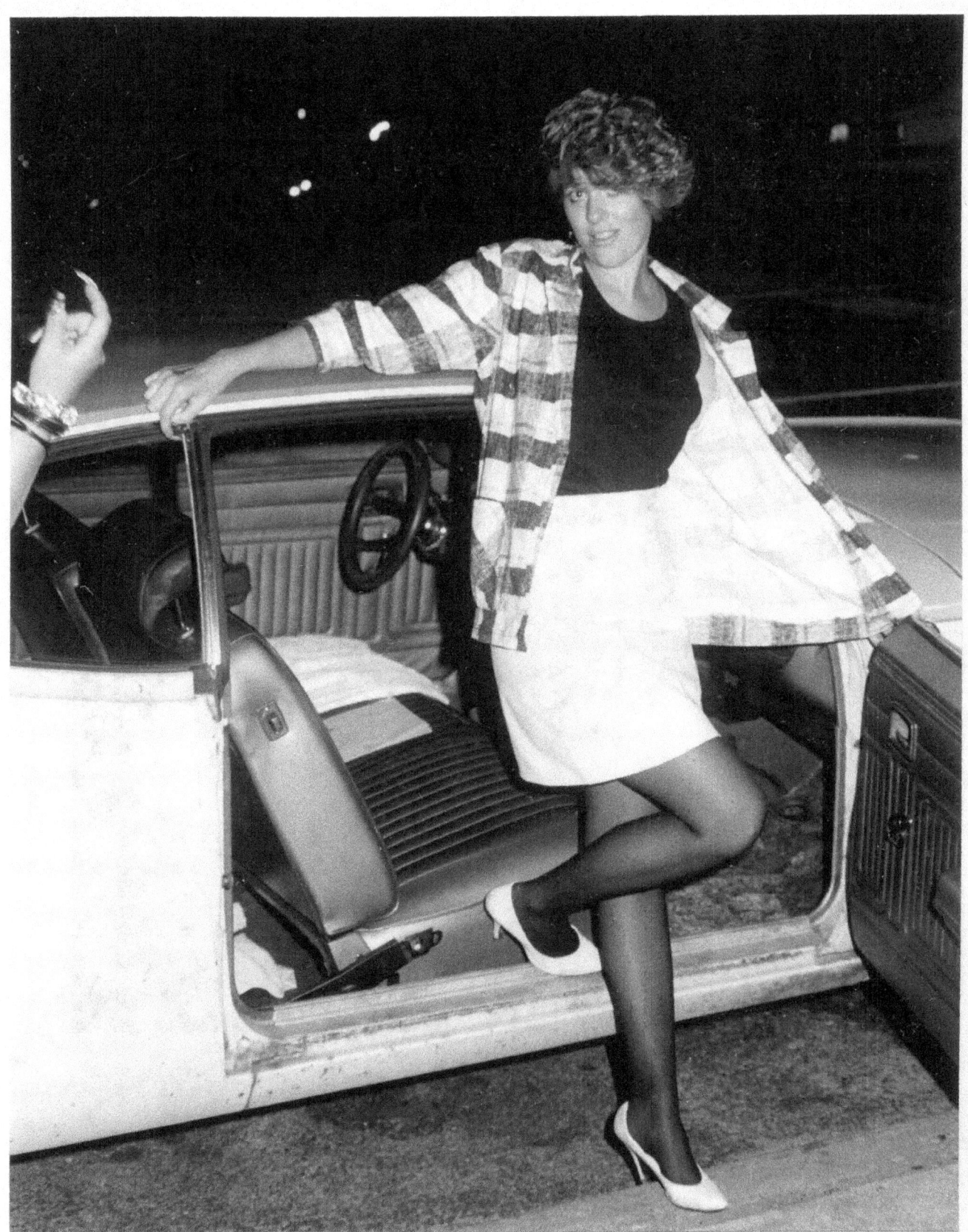

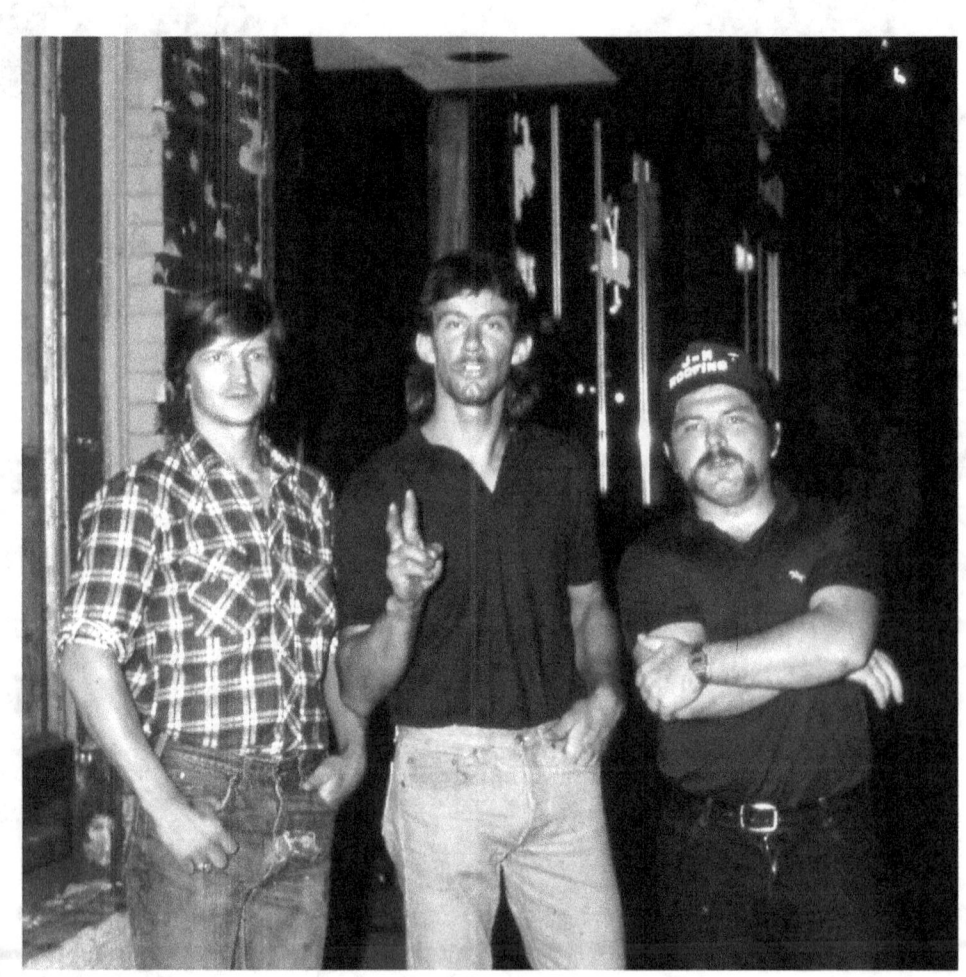

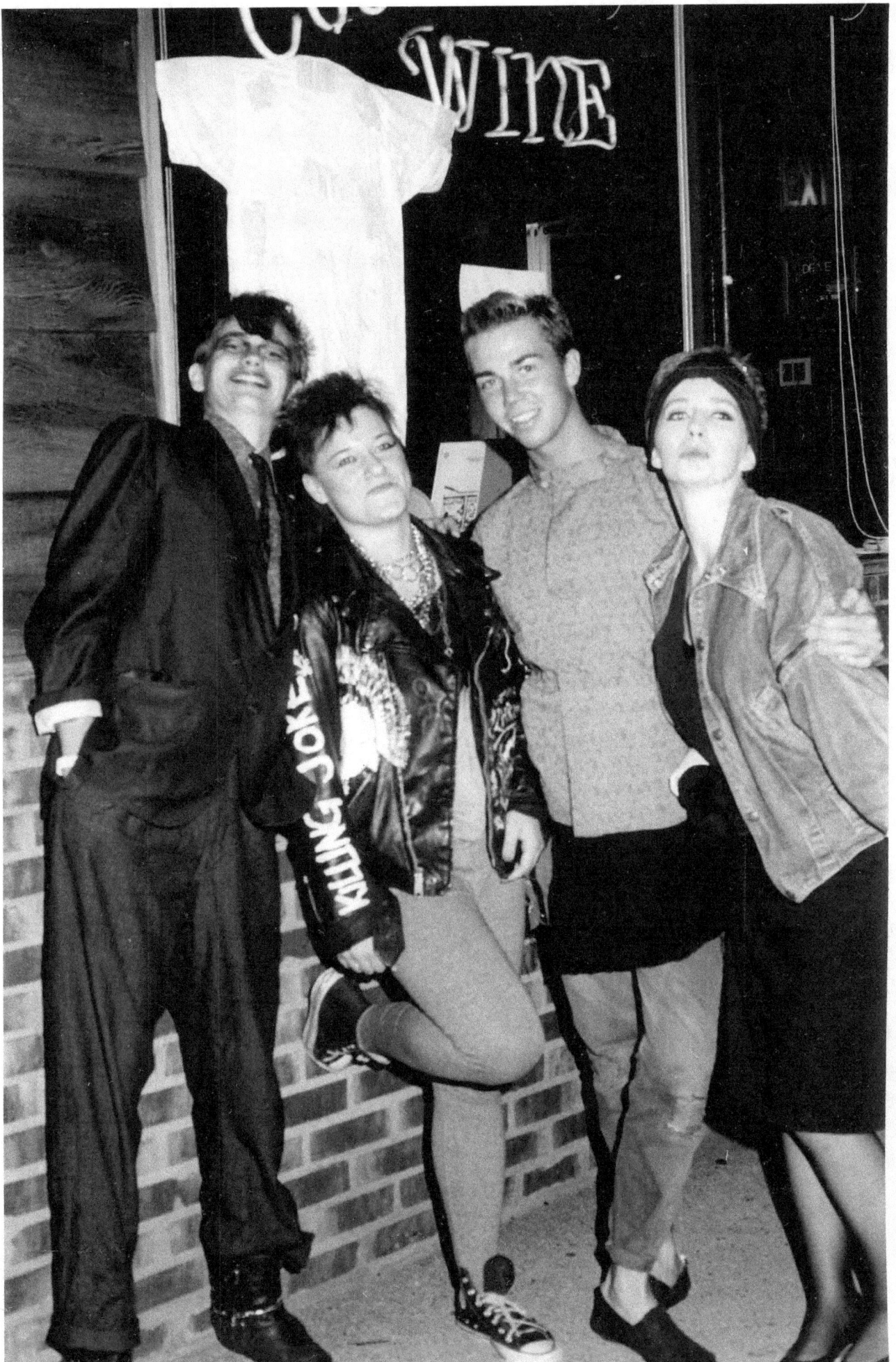

If any television, motion picture or film wants my photo. I need 10% of all.

Be some good publicity for the mad daog man, I'm a producer. Good publicity, great & free too. Record producer, not big time but I know a few of the big shots.

That's killer man, that's killer, that's killer. Your doing your own thing just like I do mine, that's killer.

Do this up right, I know I'm being a conceded son of a bitch but I've been here since seven-thirty tonight. I ain't got nobody to fuckin dance with me. I ain't got nobody to do jack shit, and I'm a fuckin professional!

Should I do my collar up or what? This suckers got so many buttons on it!

This chick reminds me of my grandmother, this one on the right she does! Hey my grandmothers killer though. She reminds me of what the hells her name? Edith Bunker.

I tried getting that little blond to go out with me tonight, she wouldn't do it. This one here, the miniskirt. Boy reminds me of the good ole' days back in the 60's those miniskirts.

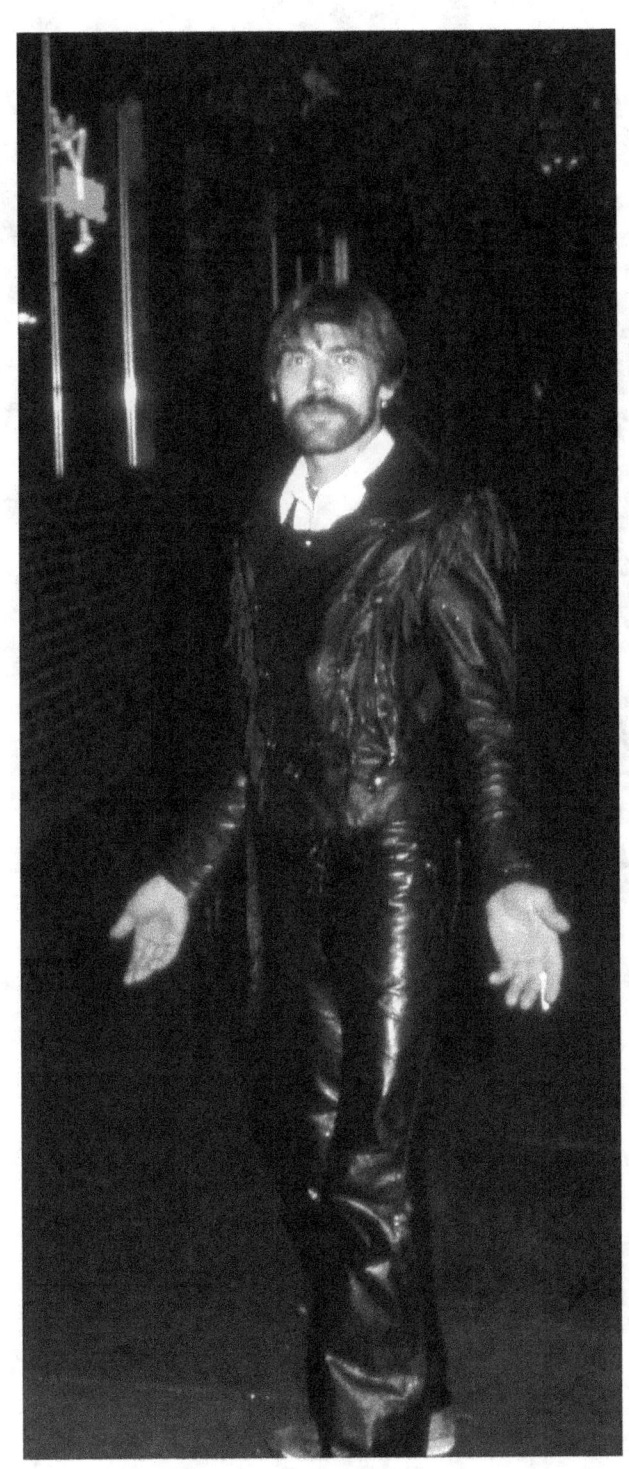

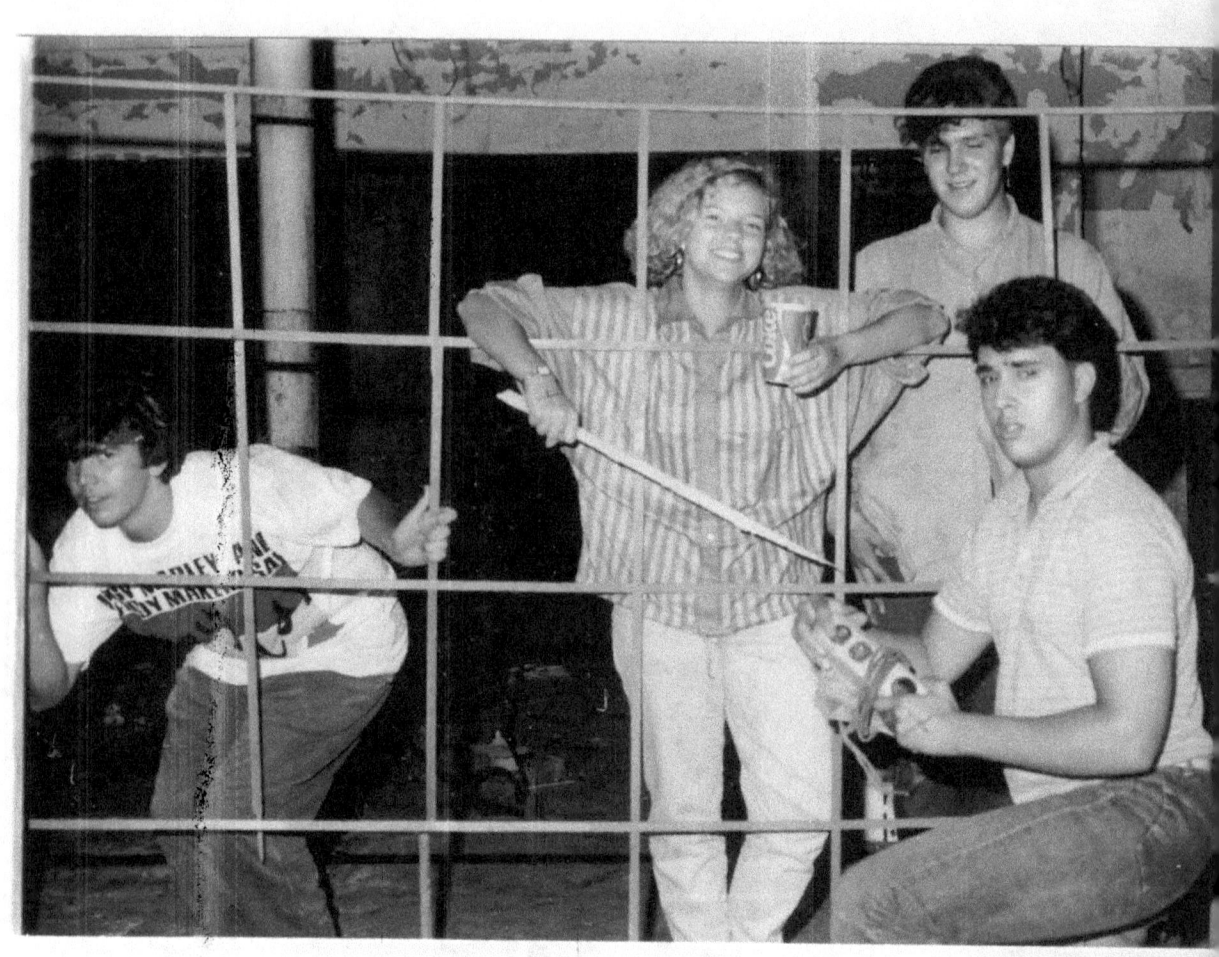

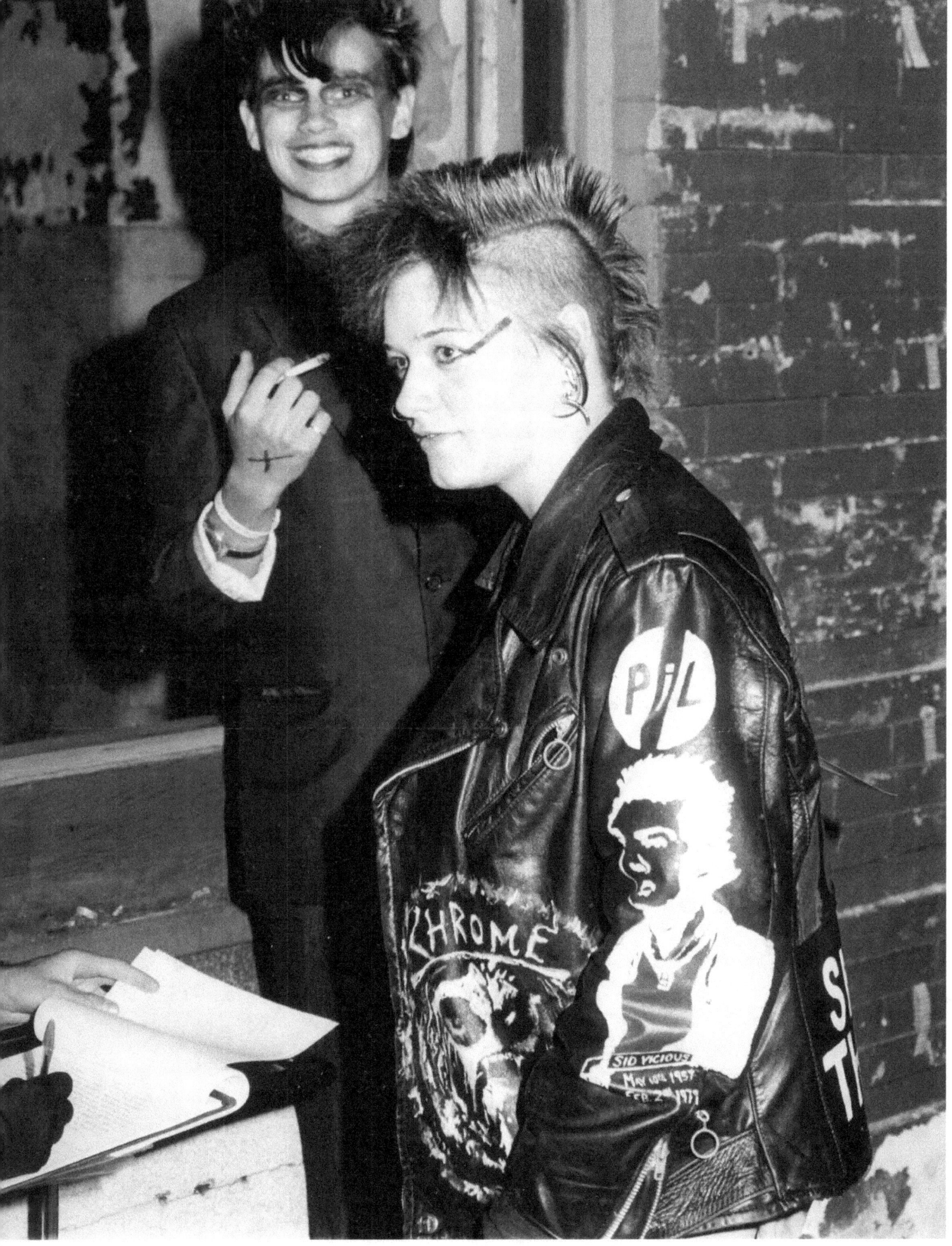

My watch is one day ahead. I like to stay one
day ahead, keeps me on schedule. Oh it's after
midnight? I must have reset it.

Of course you don't know him from the days
I know him from. They went like mad in Australia,
in fact he even made a live album in Austraalia and
I got it. It's worth fifty dollars, can't get it in
this country. Have to special order it and you've
got to know the right people. And I know the
right people, some of them anyways.

Can you get a picture like blowing smoke out?
Would that be crude you know?

Do I look nasty? I'm not drunk.

I feel like a hooker get a picture of this,
evidence for the court.

Would they be neat? Want me to ask them for you?
"Okay do you want your picture taken? No it
doesn't cost nothing just sign your name different.
People at the Club Soda man it's really cool.
Come sign the paper when your done or before".

I'm gonna put _____ _____ here.
Actually my first name is dinosaur.

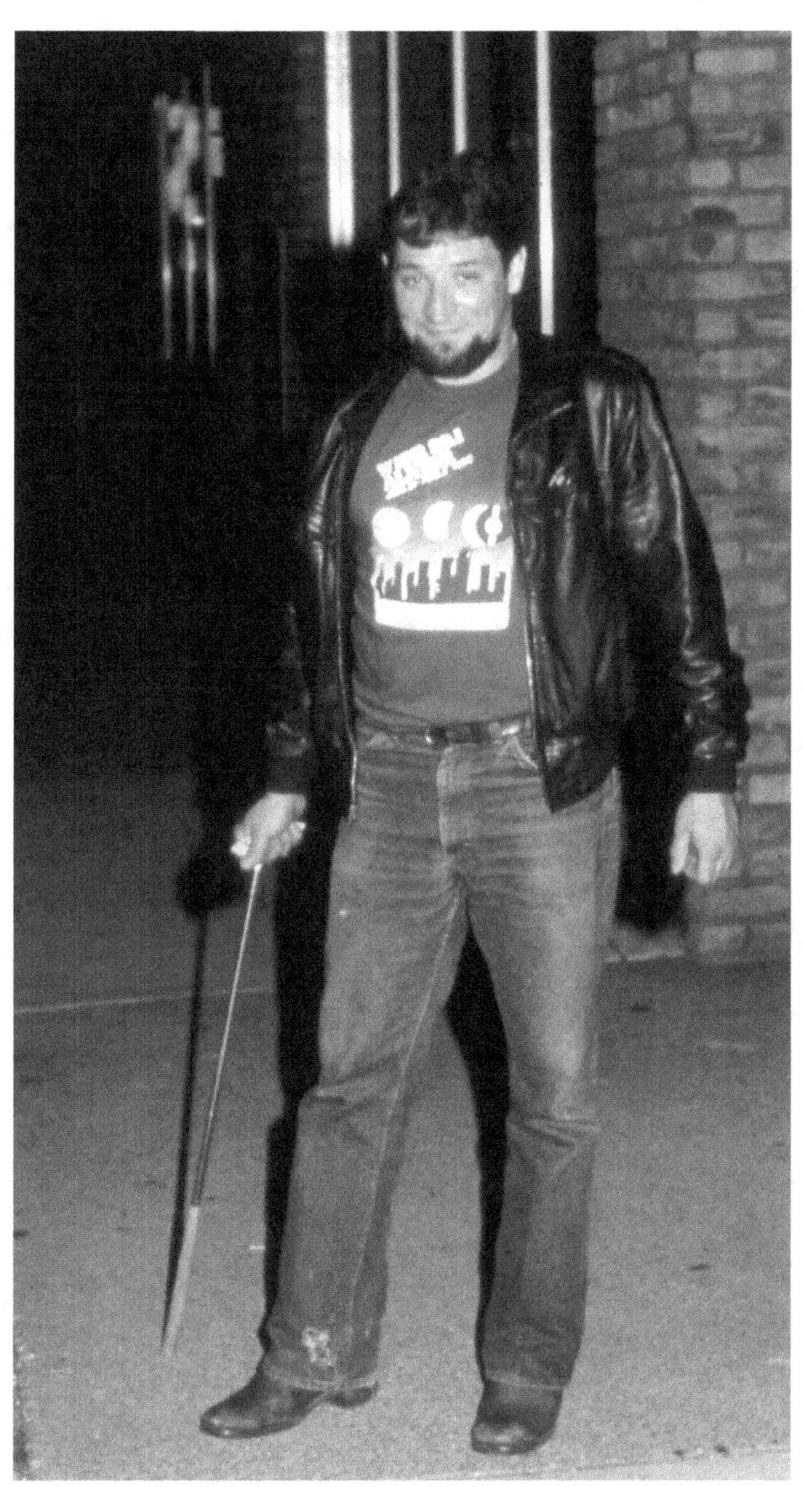

"I love I'm like a hobbyist at photography. I waste a lot of film because I don't know what I'm doing. But I come up with some really good ones. I like taking lightning pictures. I mean not as good as the ones that you see you know wide lens and this big thing in the middle but I've gotten some pretty good ones for myself and other neat things like when we've had party's and um like my roomate was down, this room was like an old garage and it was just down there and there was just one light on and he was just down there jamming out just by himself and he had a hat on and it was really dim and I took it and put it in the show at the student center. Well I just kinda do it for fun but it, I thought they were really cool. I called it "The Record Player" cause he just like would play along with what's on. And he's like, and then there's another one and he's just like- then him and his girlfriend were sitting on the bed like this and then there's a third one where they flipped over, they really turned out neat. I just wish I knew more about it but, I used to when I was in high school I got into it a lot."

I got into a miniature conversation with her and everything, it was okay.

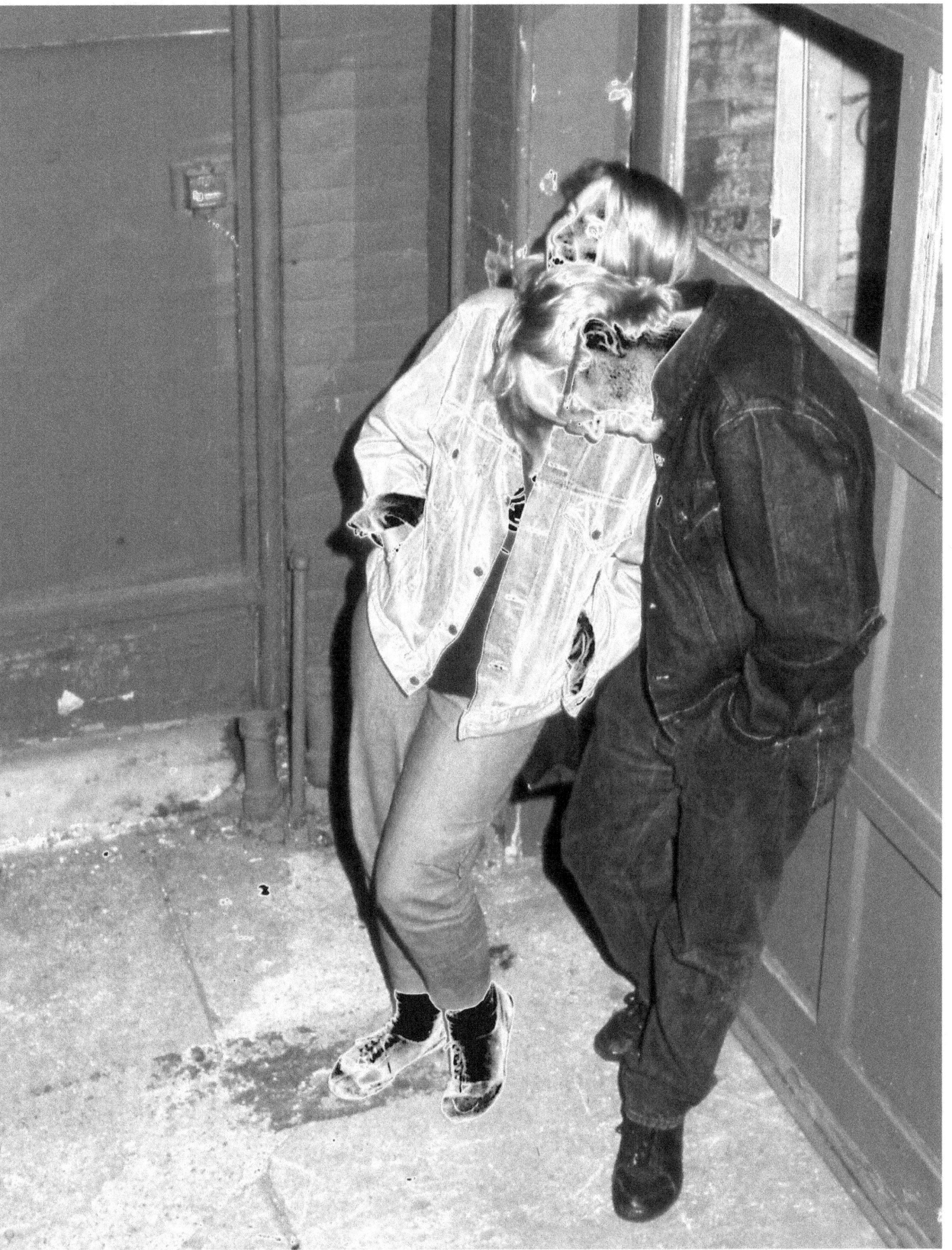

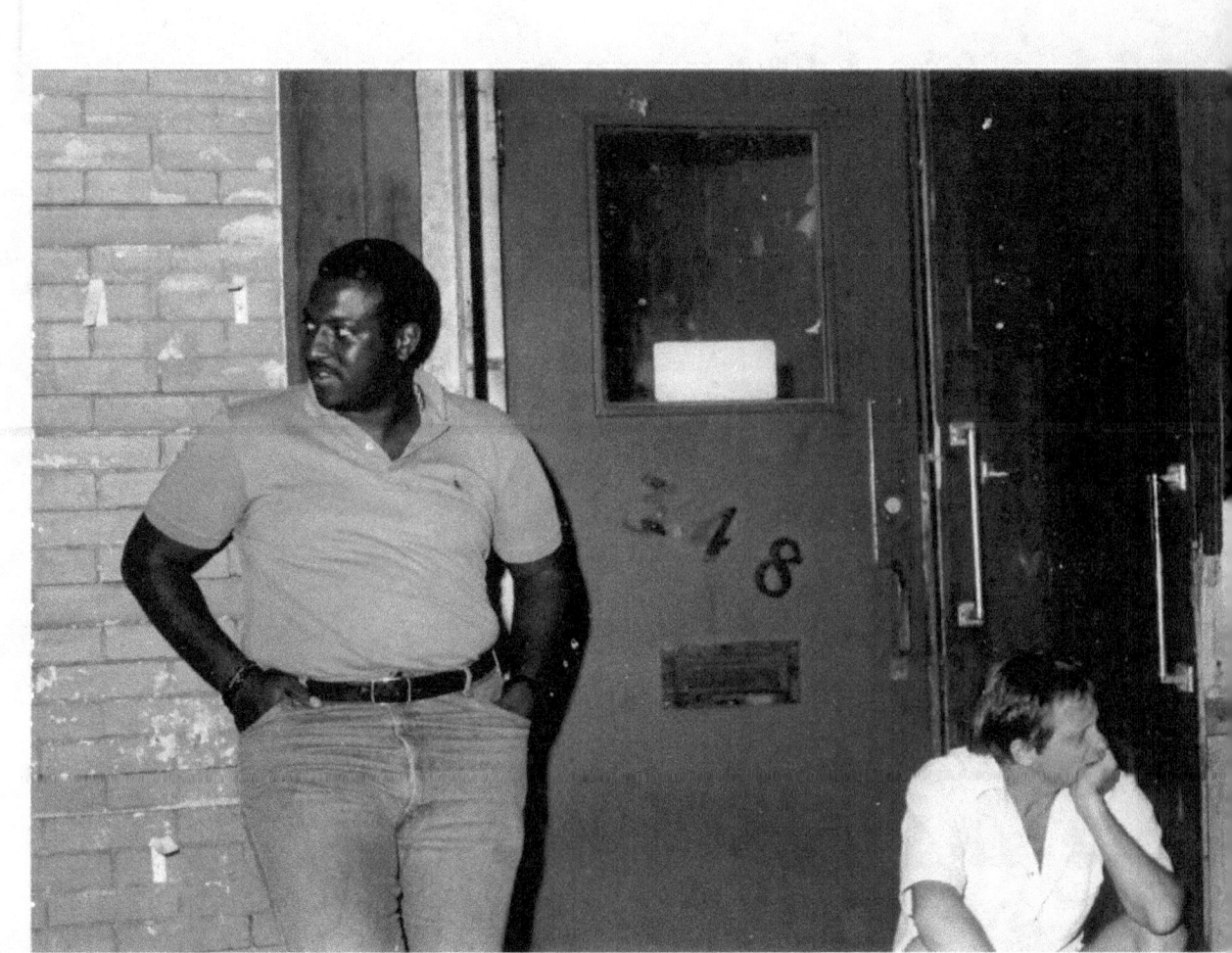

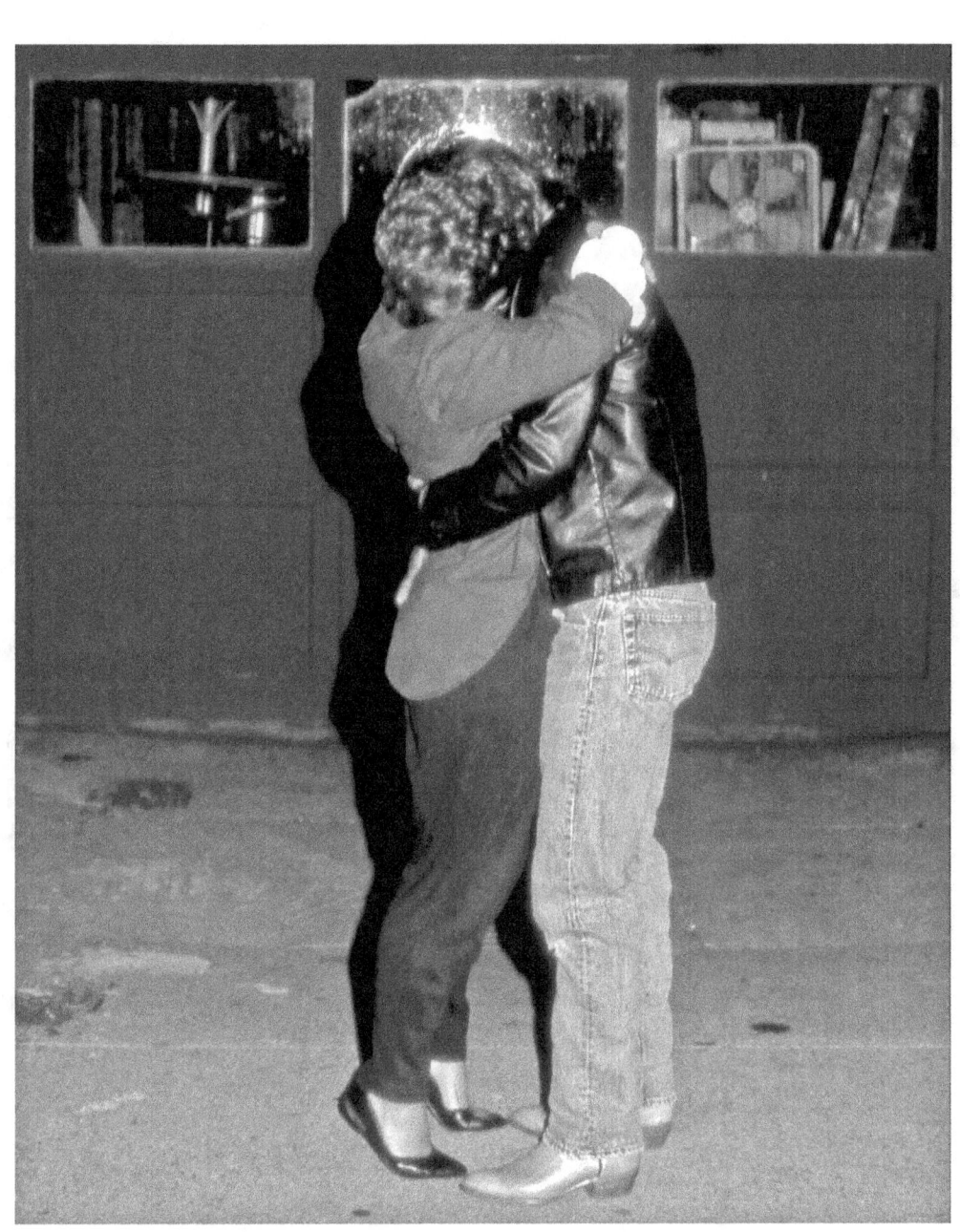

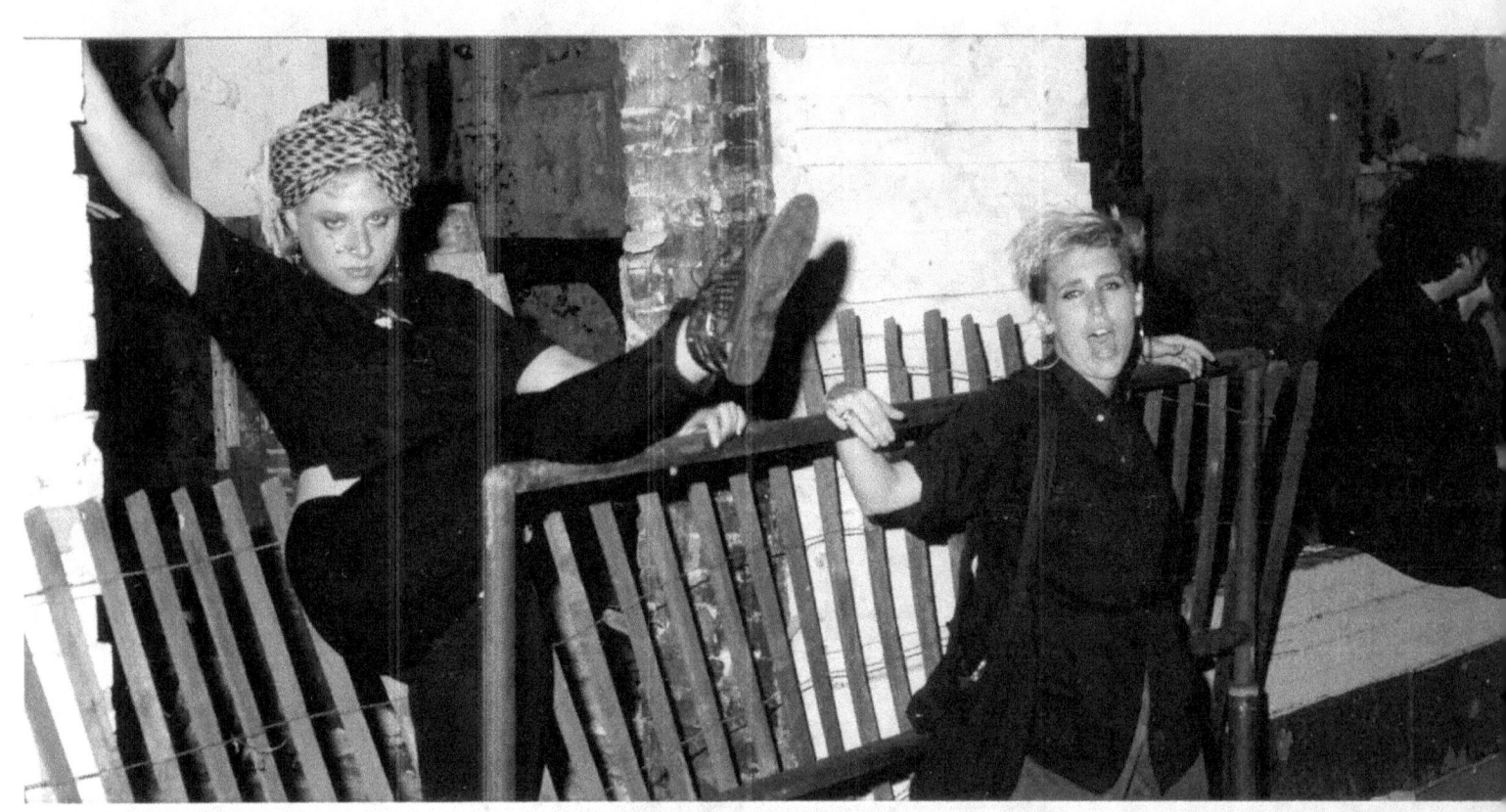

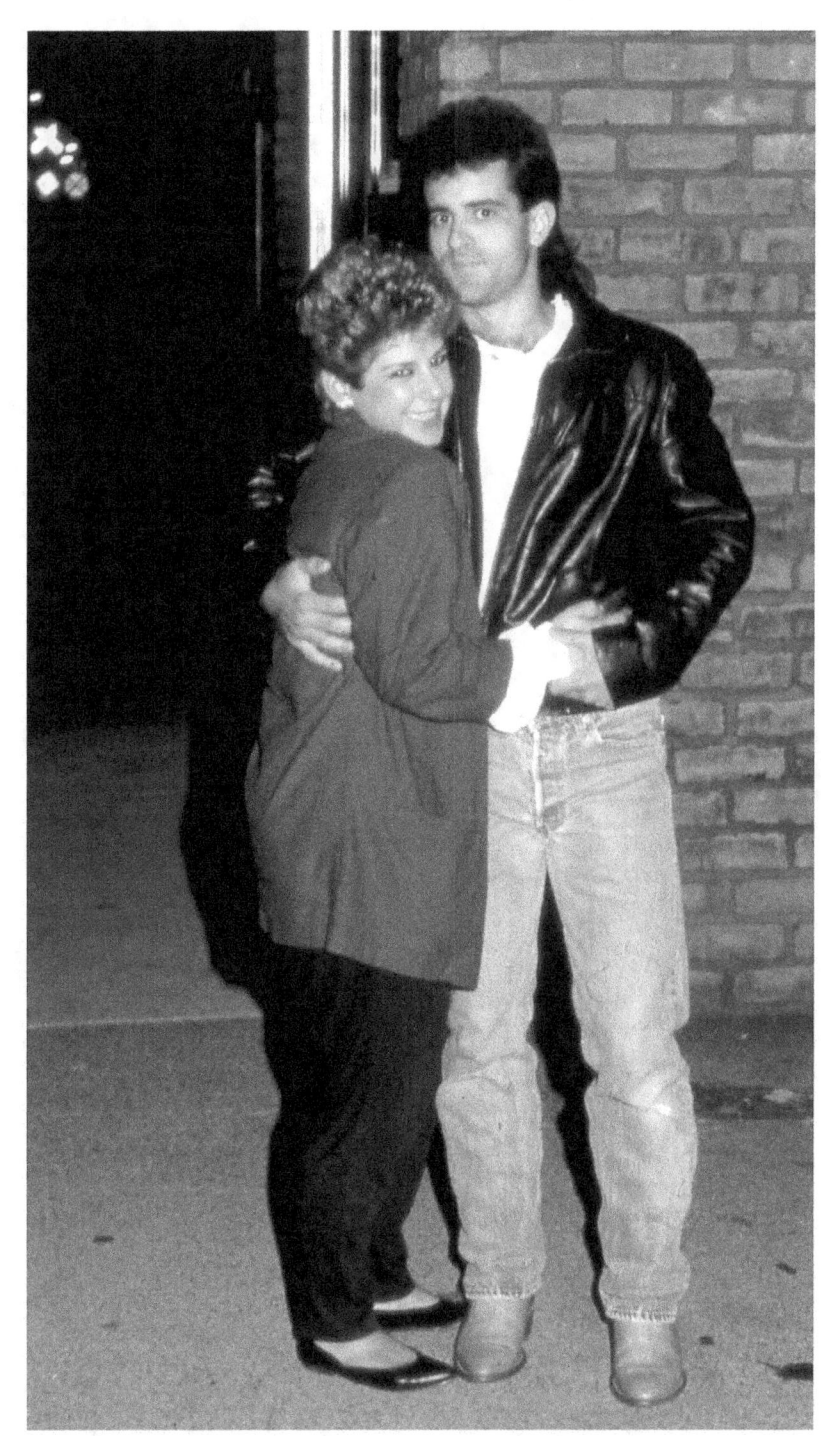

Your definently going to freeze your ass off.
It's chilly, it's like fifty-three degrees.

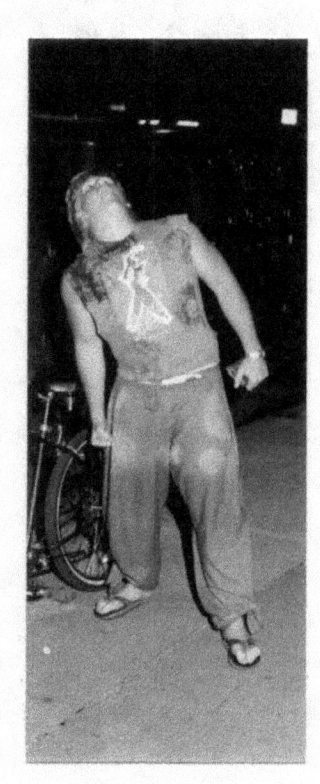

I don't know if I want to walk in that place. Everyone's going to look at us and laugh, it's like 1:05 AM.

I have a beer and I don't want to bring in my beer. Why are we walking? Muchies, we haven't eaten once and we've gone through three stages of munchies. That reefers killer.

Your gonna freeze out here.

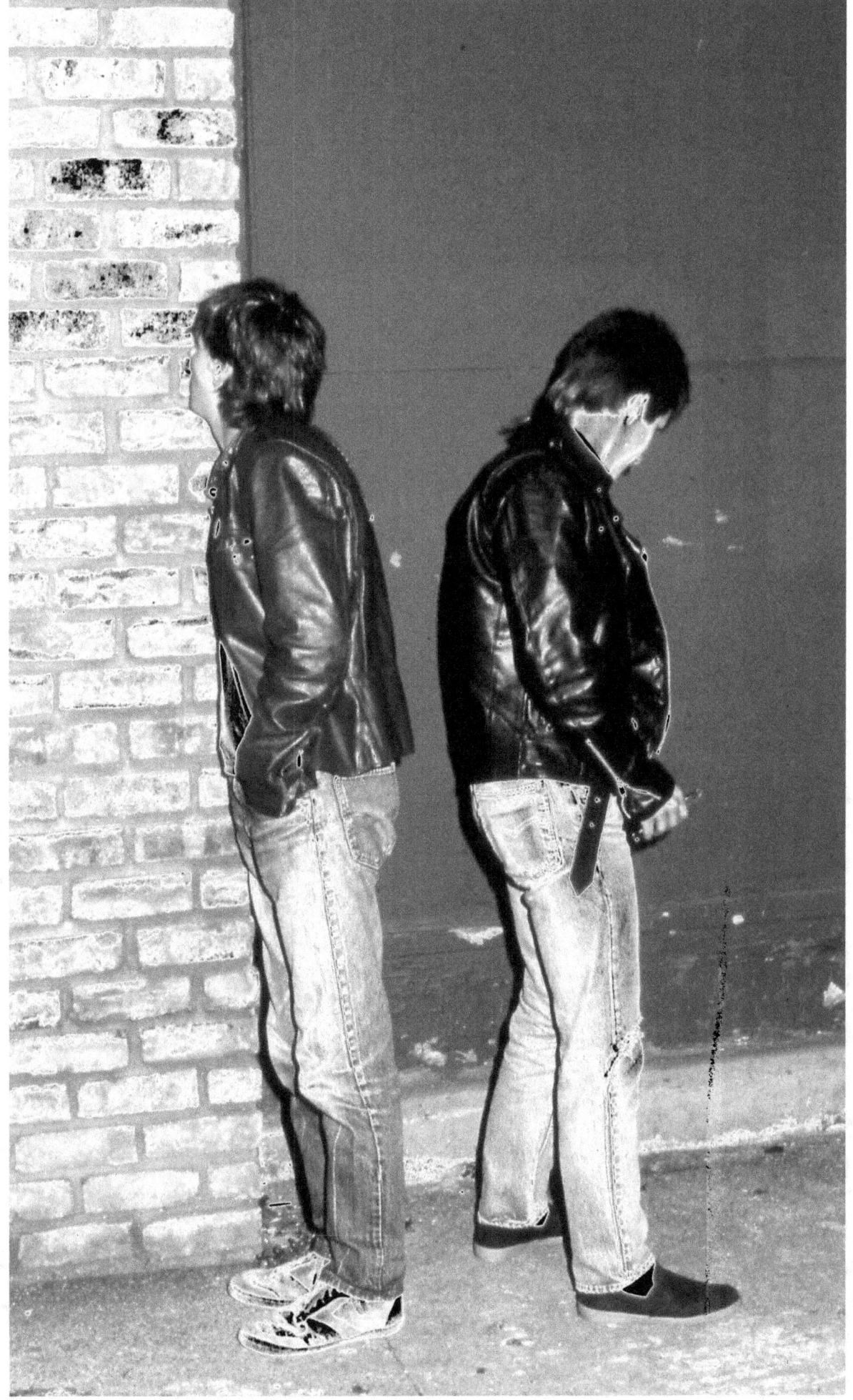

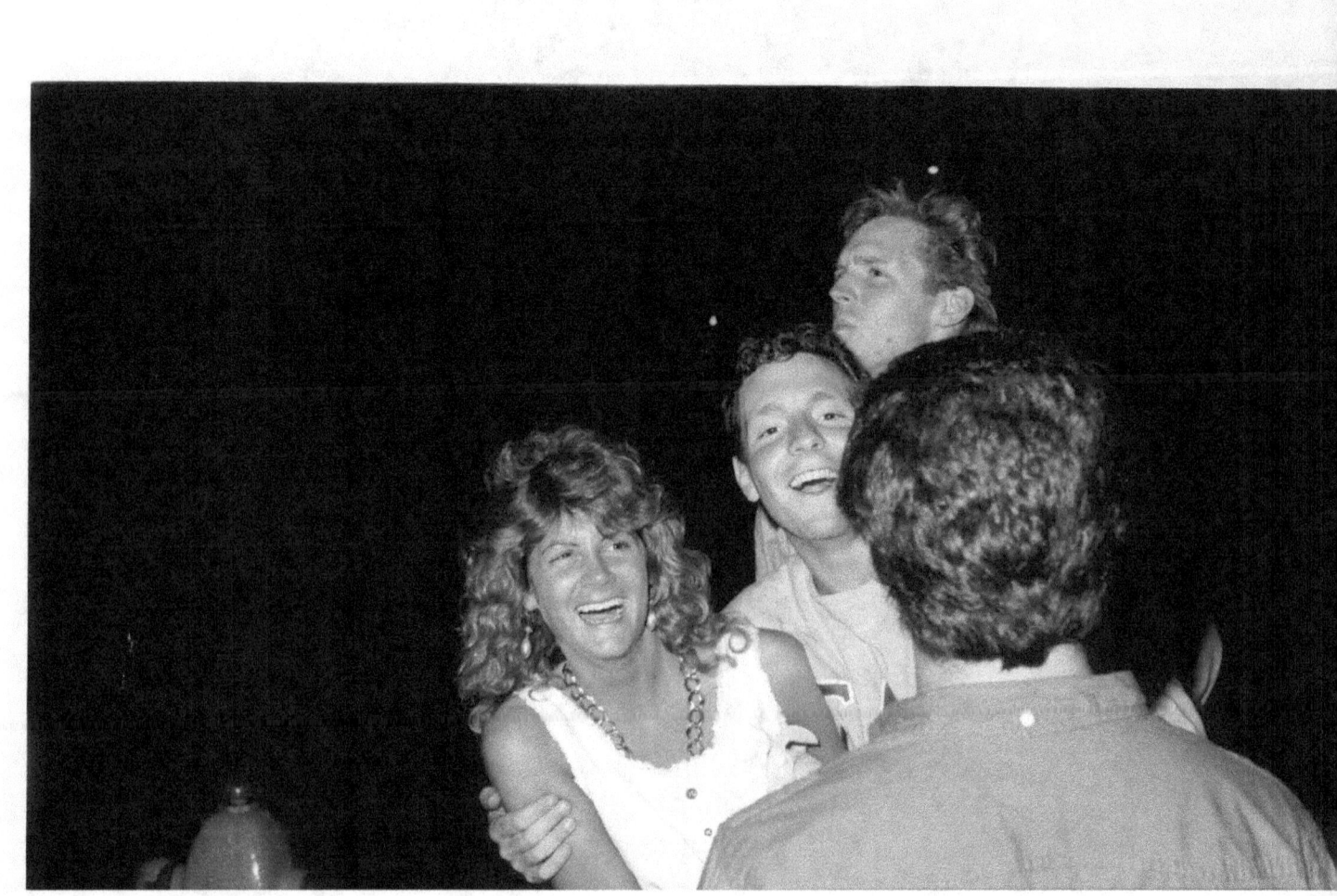

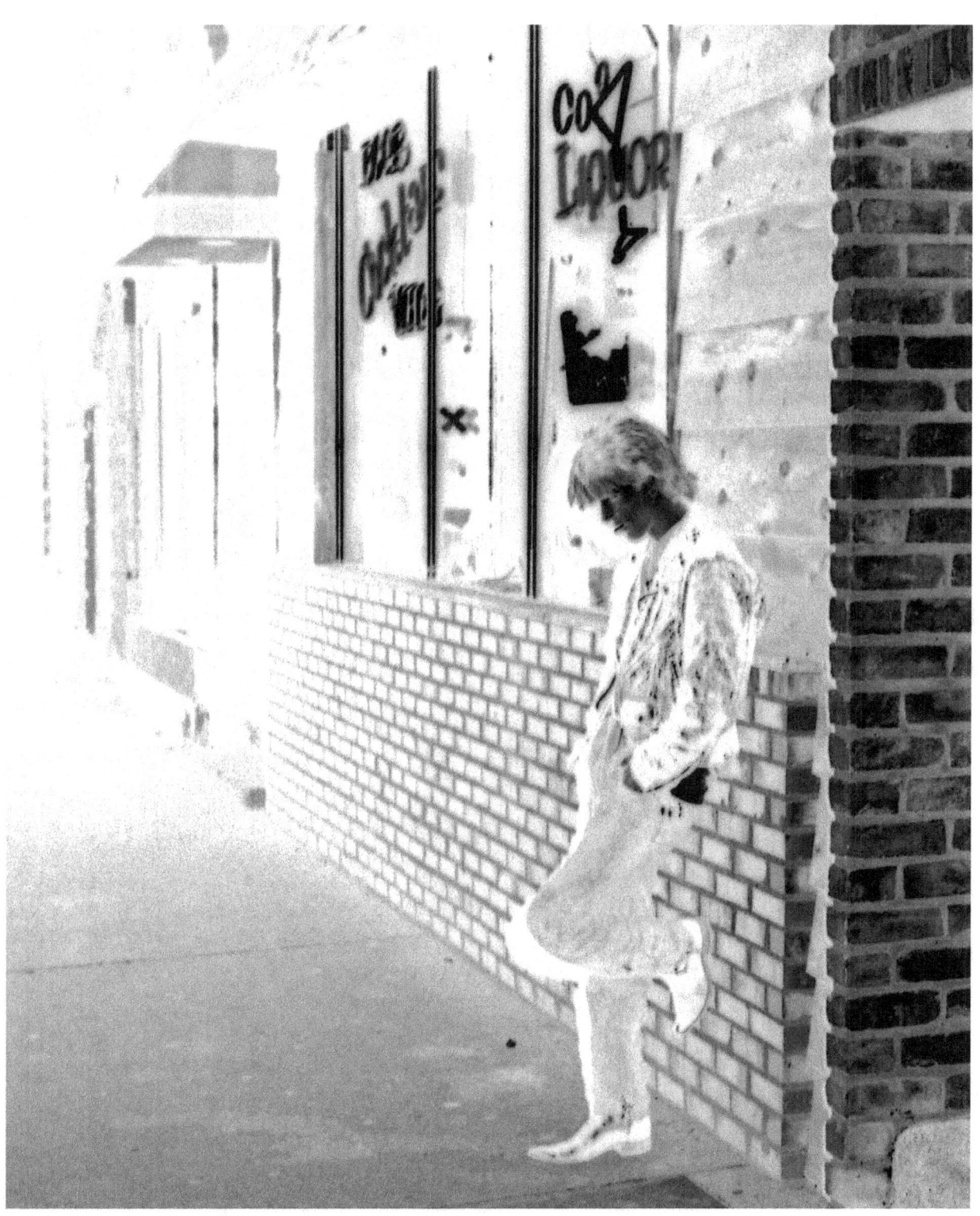

We're two Scotts, and Englishman and a Jew.

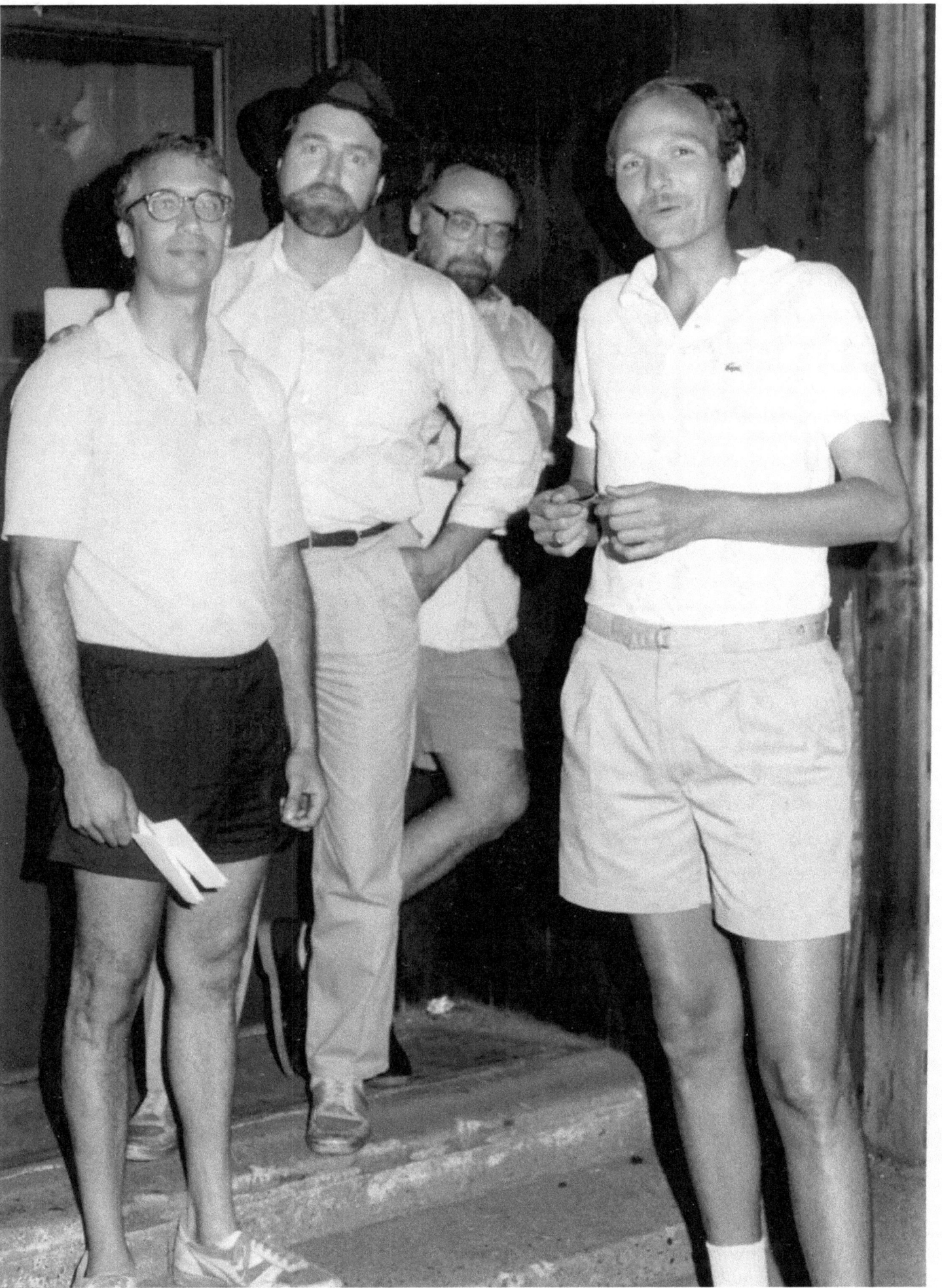

Wait let me get a cigarette.

F.A.Q. What you may ask does F.A.Q. stand for?
We don't know Fack You!
What do you think it stands for? It's just a name.
Just like C.U.T. or I.D.K. ya or Misfits,
uhuh Dead Kennedy's.

Wonder if the police will come by? Don't they
ever get you for loitering & shit?

Take any pictures of the bands? That would be cool.

Did you know who that guy in that van was?
Probably gonna wait for us and when we get to our
car they're gonna jump out with pipes and...
"Don't do that we're pacifists, really".

(on being under 21)
I don't see what good it does, why they won't let
us in. Usually you can get in bars if you get there
before eight-thirty or nine. They start checking at
nine. No big deal.

Wanna borrow my jacket? I'll come for it.

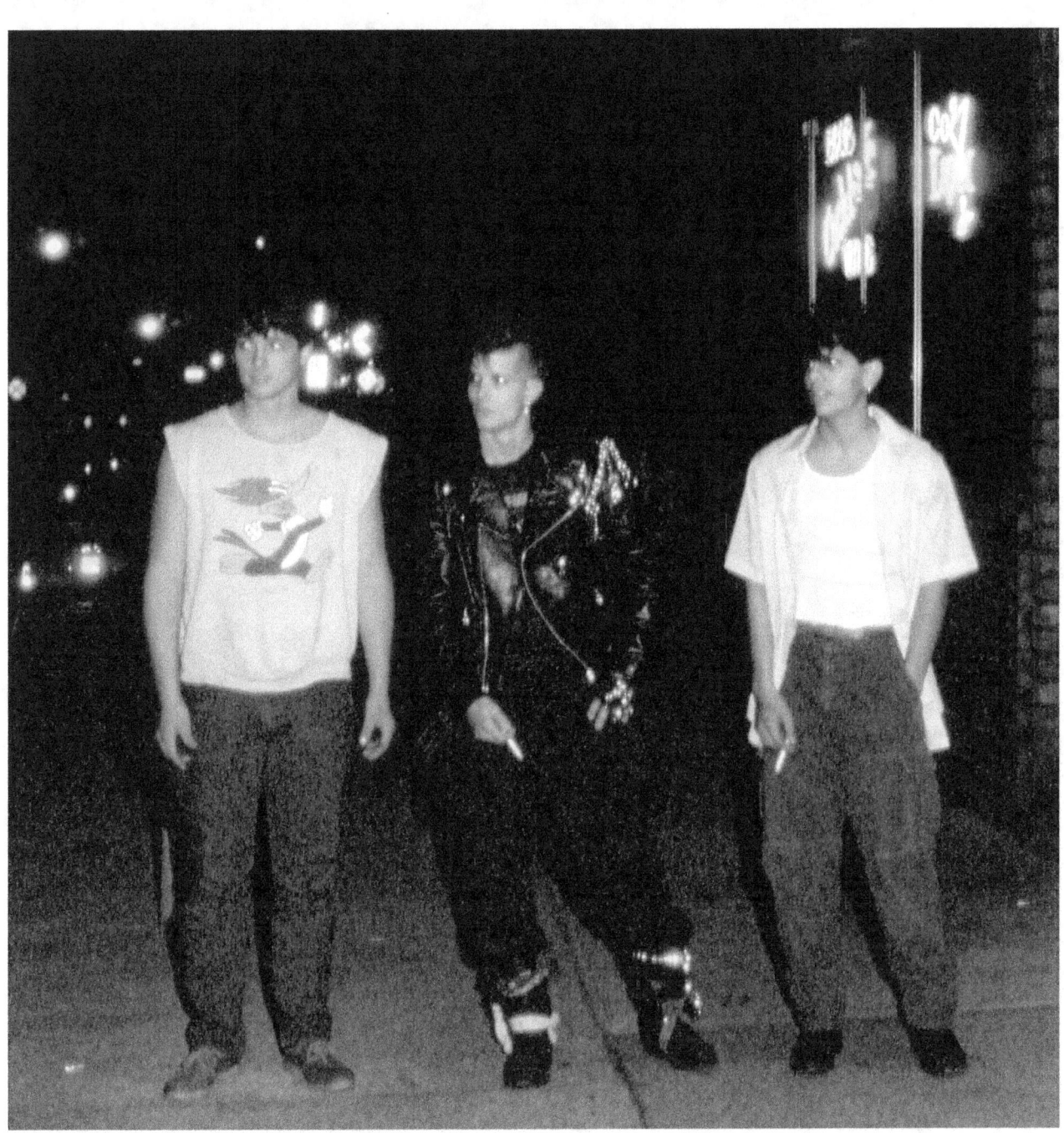

Long as I don't go to jail for it.

Wish I had my Harley down here, then I'd really enjoy it.

I guess I'll give it this time, I usually charge for this shit.

My cousin is going back to Iowa tomorrow and we said we'd meet him out here, a few more minutes then say fuck it. It's pretty bad, they've got way to much power and all the music sounds the same. I'm pretty open minded when it comes to music but this shit is shit.

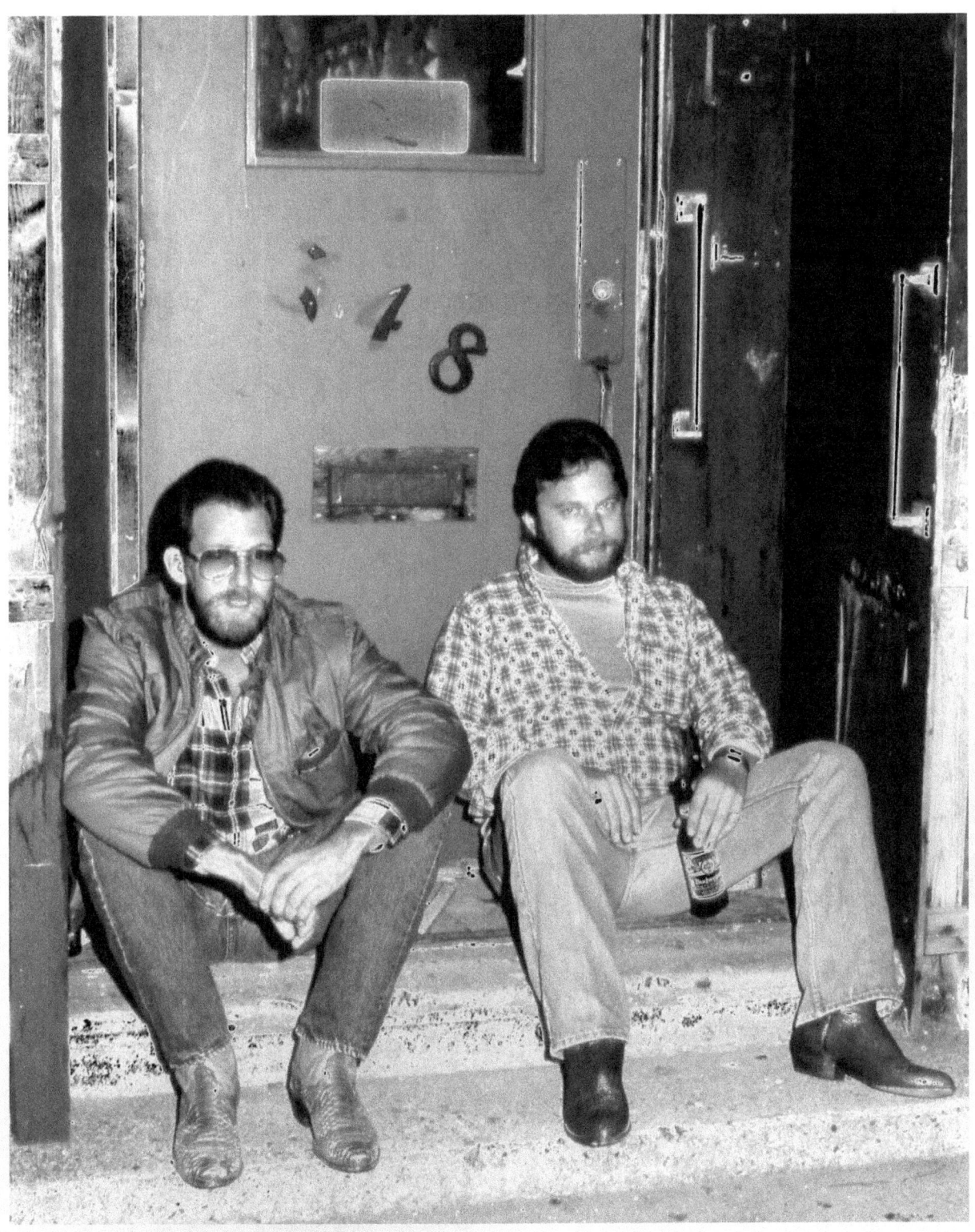

I've taken tons of pictures inside there and I've got like about a portfolio of pictures inside that hotel and the place is great!
You can walk in the door down there, really neat inside. Upstairs it's got like three stories or four? You can count yourself but there's like about eighty rooms and the rooms are incredible there's all this water damage so it's just like these incredible shapes. It's all rusted out and there's like these sliding metal doors in between the hallways that they had in like ah, Texas Chainsaw Massacre you know that metal doorway that goes whaaaam! you know. It's really old it's like 1890 architecture, it's incredible. We shot about, we've been up there about four different times with a camera. One time with a super-8 and one time with a 35 and those things just came out incredible because at that time it was about a year ago and I was like bondage and my girlfriend who was in the band with me was like white you know. So the pictures came out really good we've used them a lot.

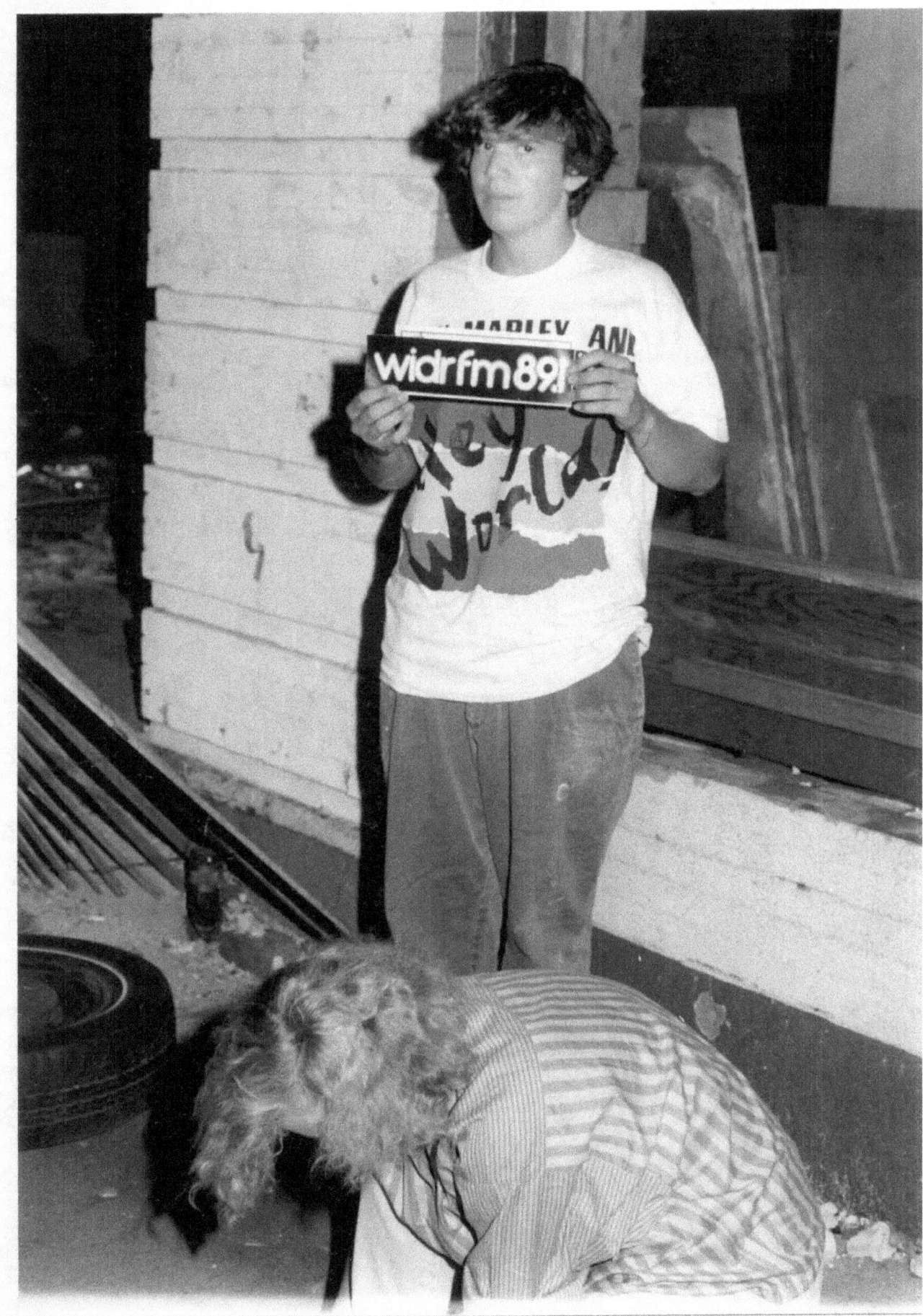

Is that a mirror? I thought it was a mirror for coke or something.

How would you like an extra schedule for music on the mall?

So, who are you like pushing these photographs to? Parent or guardian? No I'm afraid not.

Well hey I hope you don't freeze to death.

-" do you have the keys?"
" no, -no, what am I supposed to do with them?"
-" you got them I hope"
" oh your right"
-" that would be a bummer, sit out here taking pictures with um?"
" okay what am I supposed to do with them?"
-" UN-LOCK THE DOOR!"

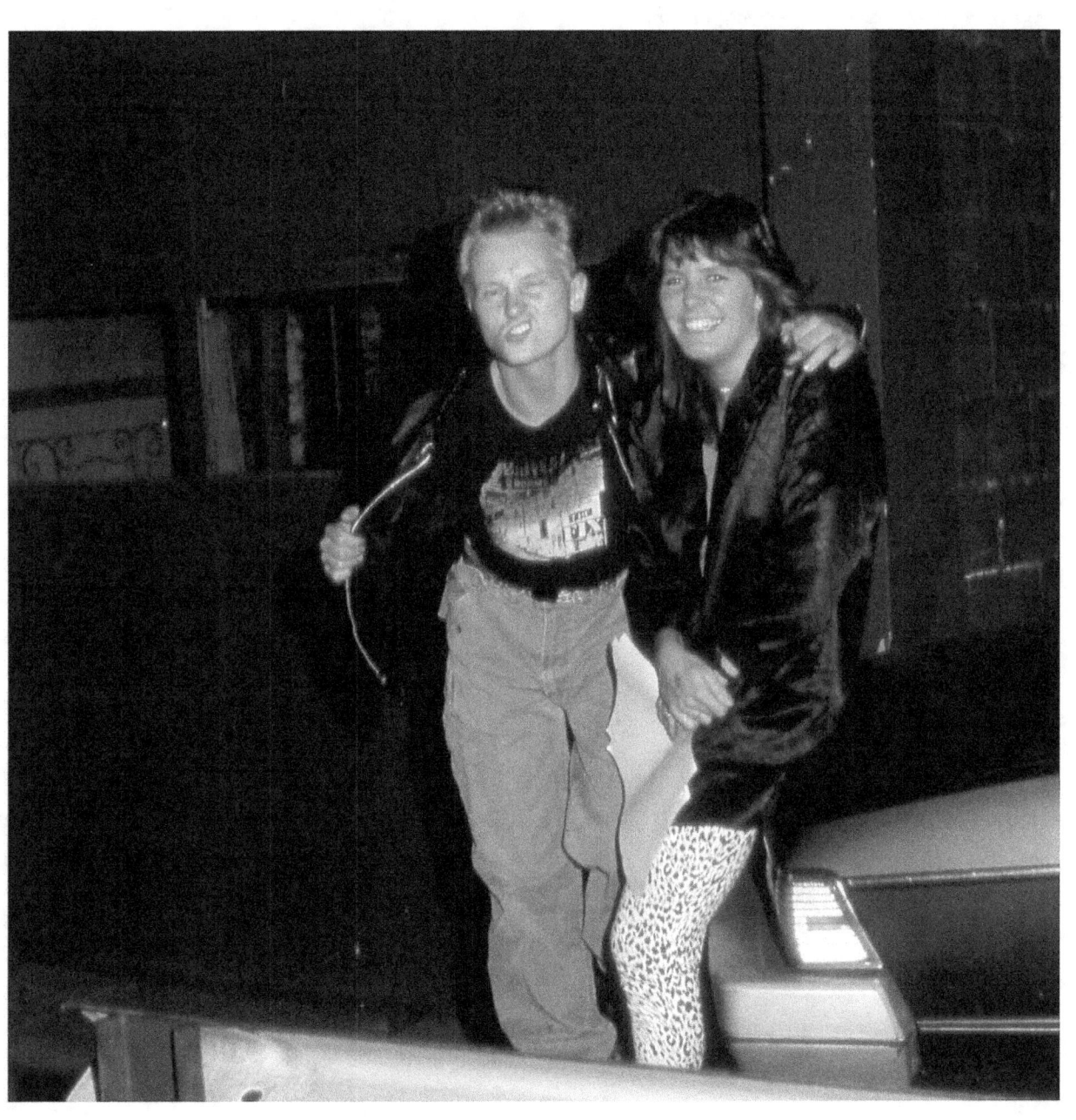

I won't sign it. I won't sue you. You don't have to worry about me. I mean, I don't even have to sign it. I mean it's not a, well obviously I'm letting you take my picture so.
I want to tell you.
I have a fear of camera's.

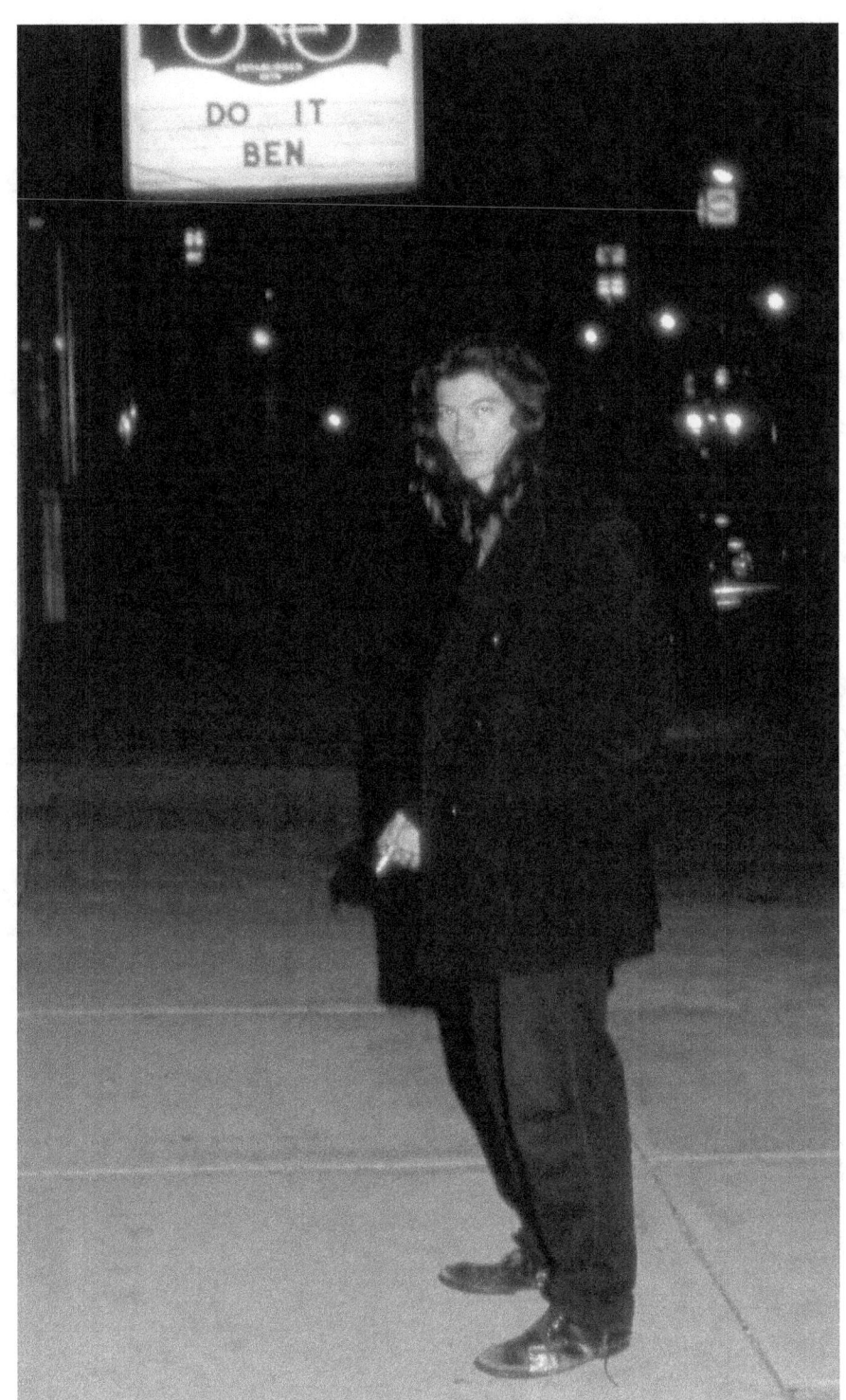

Give me two dollars and I'll let you take as many as you want.

Yeah I'll let you publish it. I'll probably look really weird, these are your photo's? Let me see if I like your work first. I'm going to be in that book America, you know that book they're doing. Life in America or whatever it's called?
It's that thing they're doing that like taking these pictures and doing a big book with it, yeah and they have like a photographer in every state.
Oh god this is really good, do it, I love it!

Well I want to go back in and drink my beer. I haven't payed for one drink and I got in for two dollars. Really and a pair of sunglasses that I bought to...

I want to be behind this, let me get rid of my purse.

She's a model anyway, everybody wants her picture. It's so weird.

She only wants my penis, she can't haver my penis because I don't have one.

Low life scums of the earth.

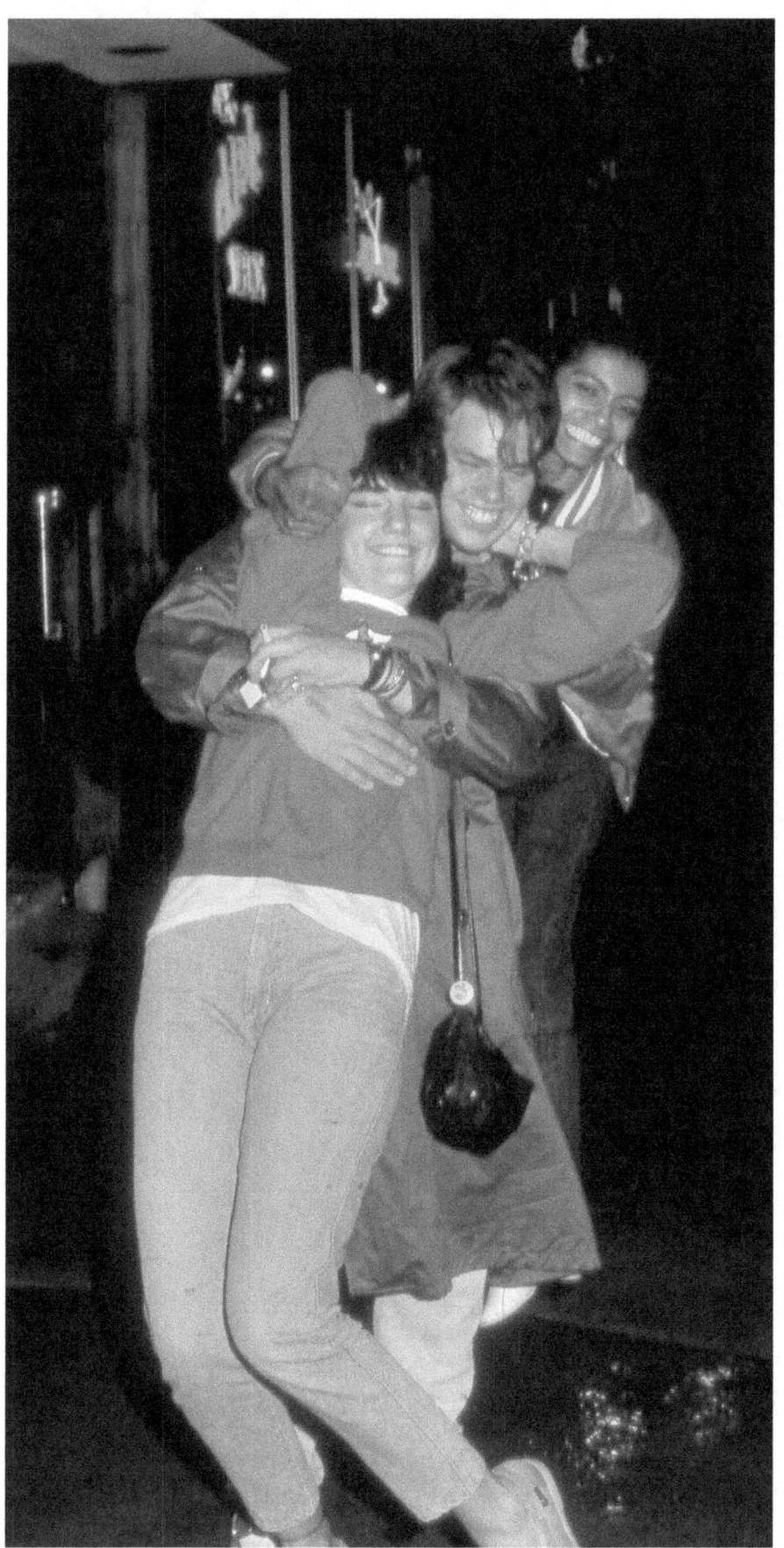

Don't you want close ups of our beautiful faces?

I'll sign for her," please excuse Jimmy from nursury school"...

People at the club are not quite mainstream, their a little different.

The Wild Woody's their okay. It gets a little old. I've seen them six or seven times, it hasn't changed. Not that somebody has to change.

Obviously taking pictures is a very personal thing.

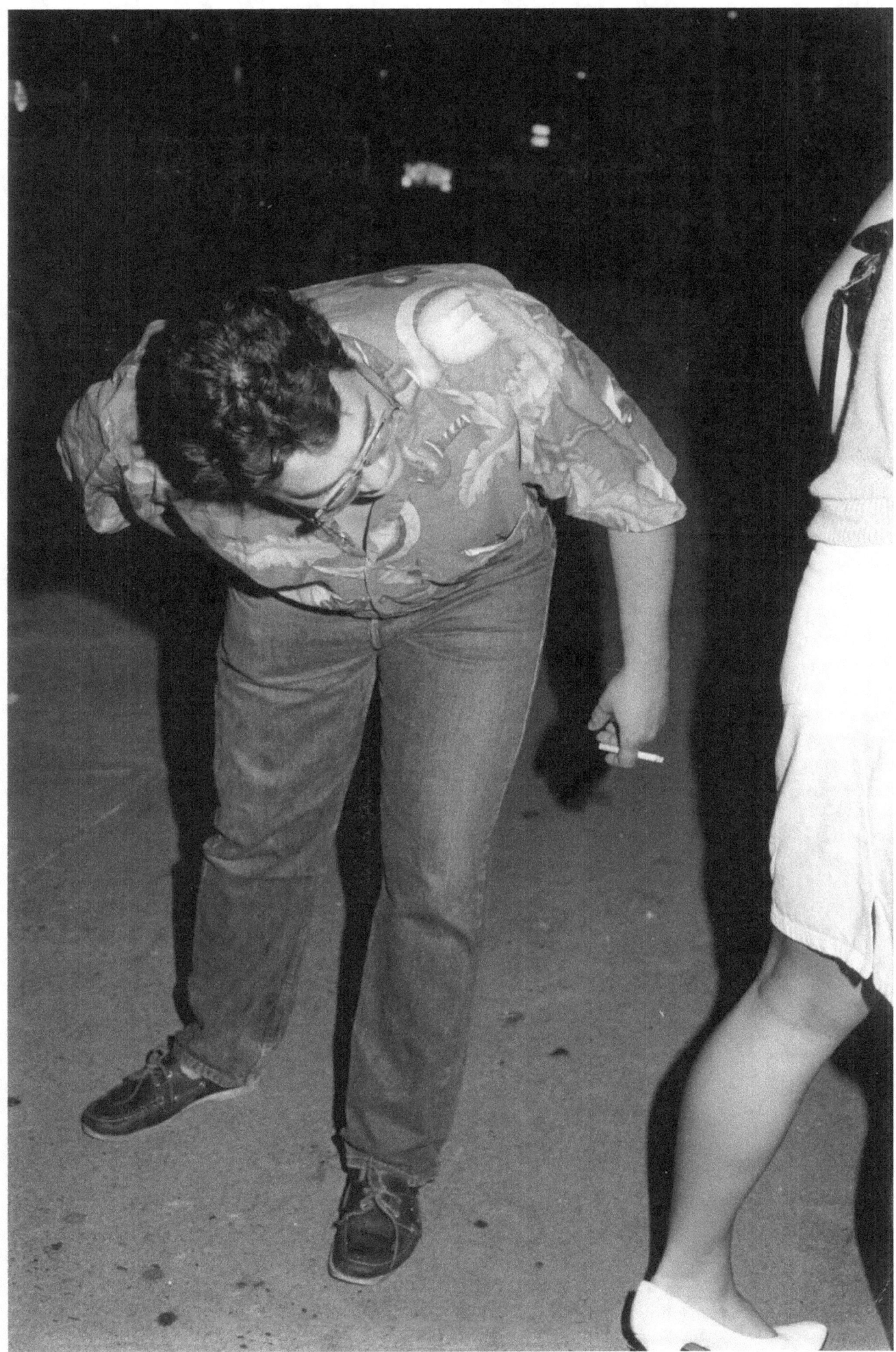

You need a caddy, an umbrella caddy or something, a lens caddy.

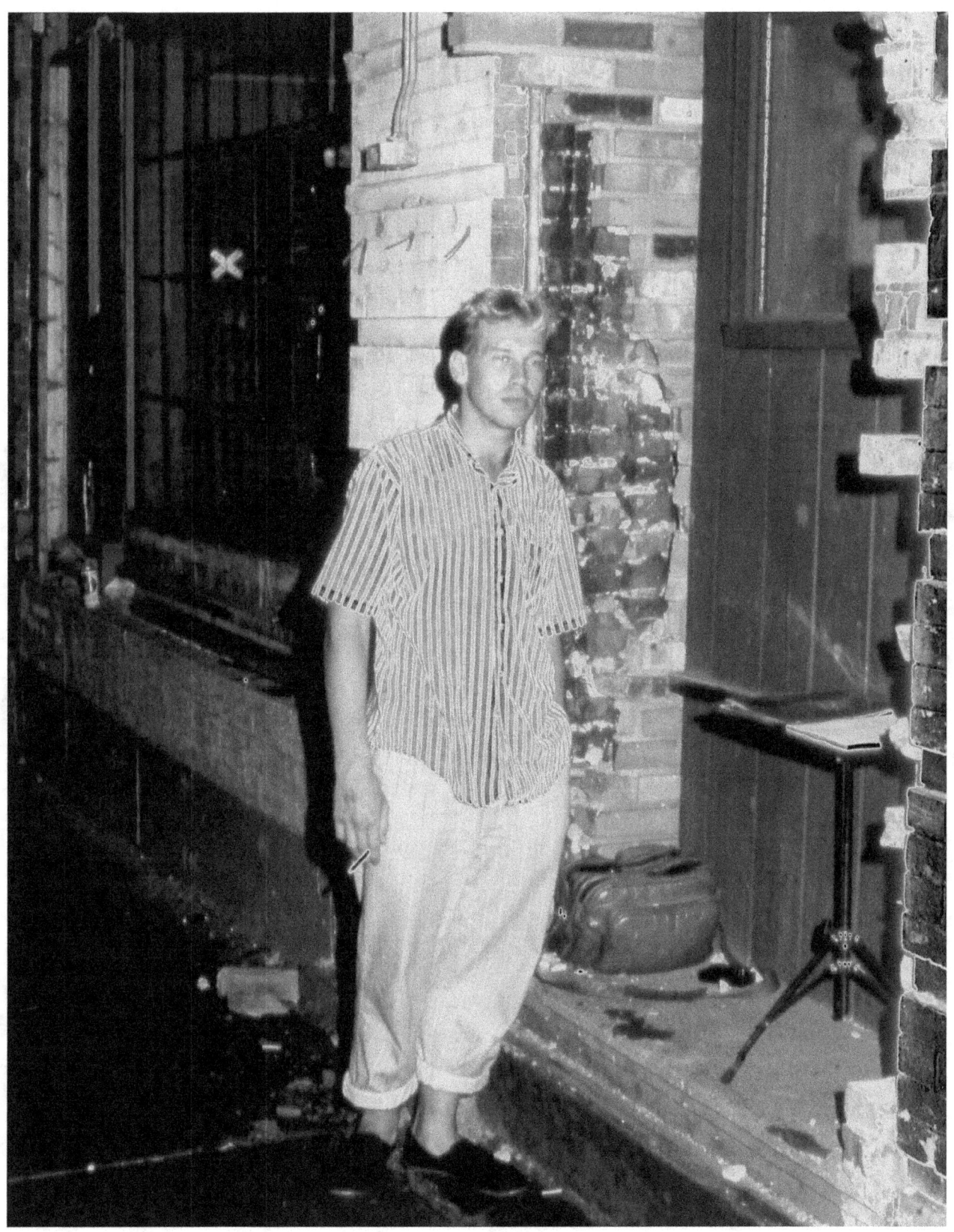

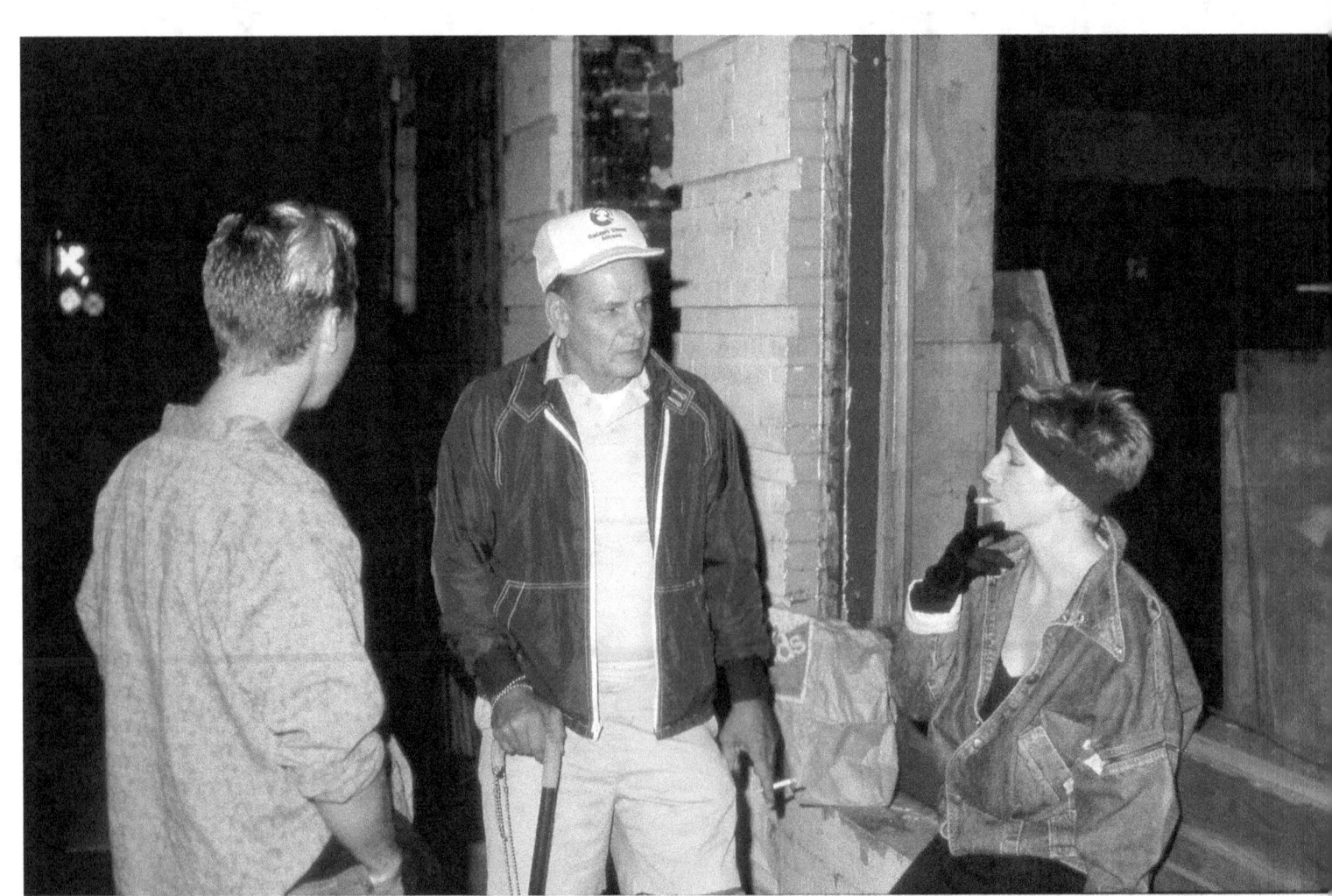

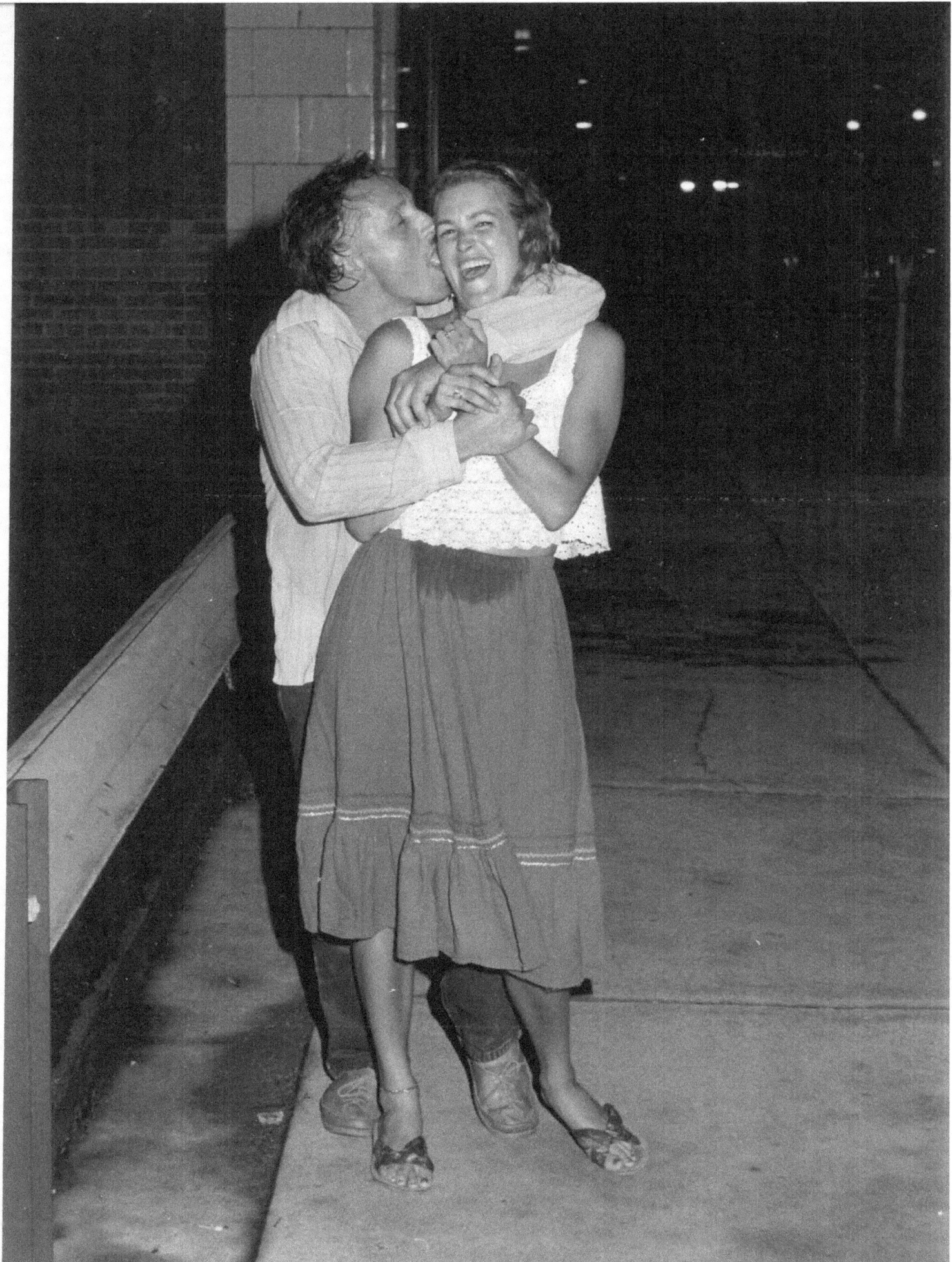

Isn't that a good signature? I should be a doctor you know.

Hey that was fun!

People are going to love it.

Very androgenous looking young lady.

Happy-go-lucky Las Vegas looking guy.

I've got a great nose.

This is great, this is such a fucking good idea man.

Tons of different stuff like on Sunday nights they go disco & stuff. Lots of different music that's why I like this place it's the best in town really.

The chicks are starting to roll in, I think I might go back in now.

Rule of thumb is: "ugly women need loving too".

People are so vain though, sometimes.

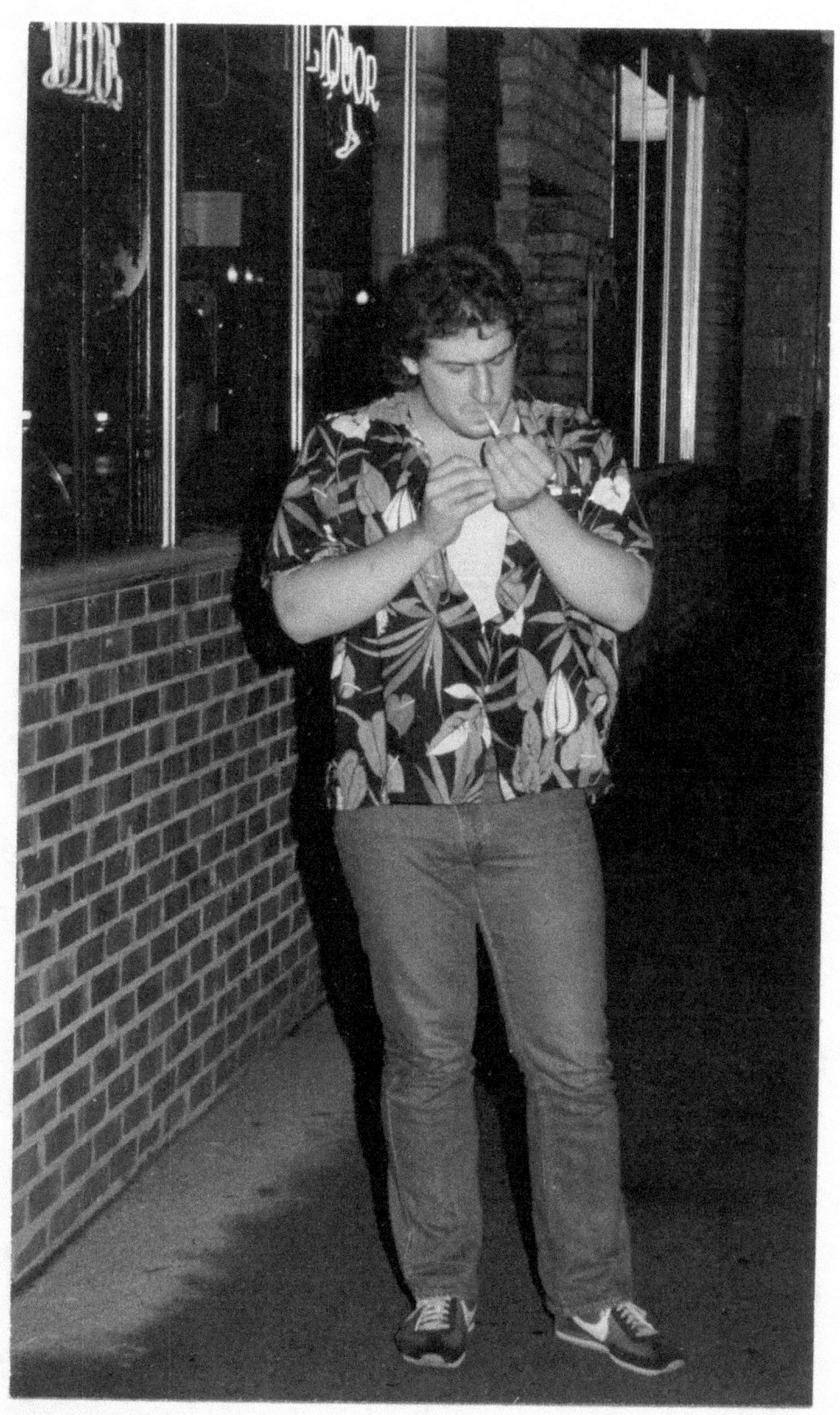

She was here, she bopped in and just went right home because I think….those guys are going over.

I'm not going to sue Bo'del we're friends from way back.

There are all sorts of body types in the world.

This body needs a lot of improvement.

I was feeling stifled in there and the attitude is not good. All last week all I did was work, the energy just abounds it felt so good. My job you know I just live for it!

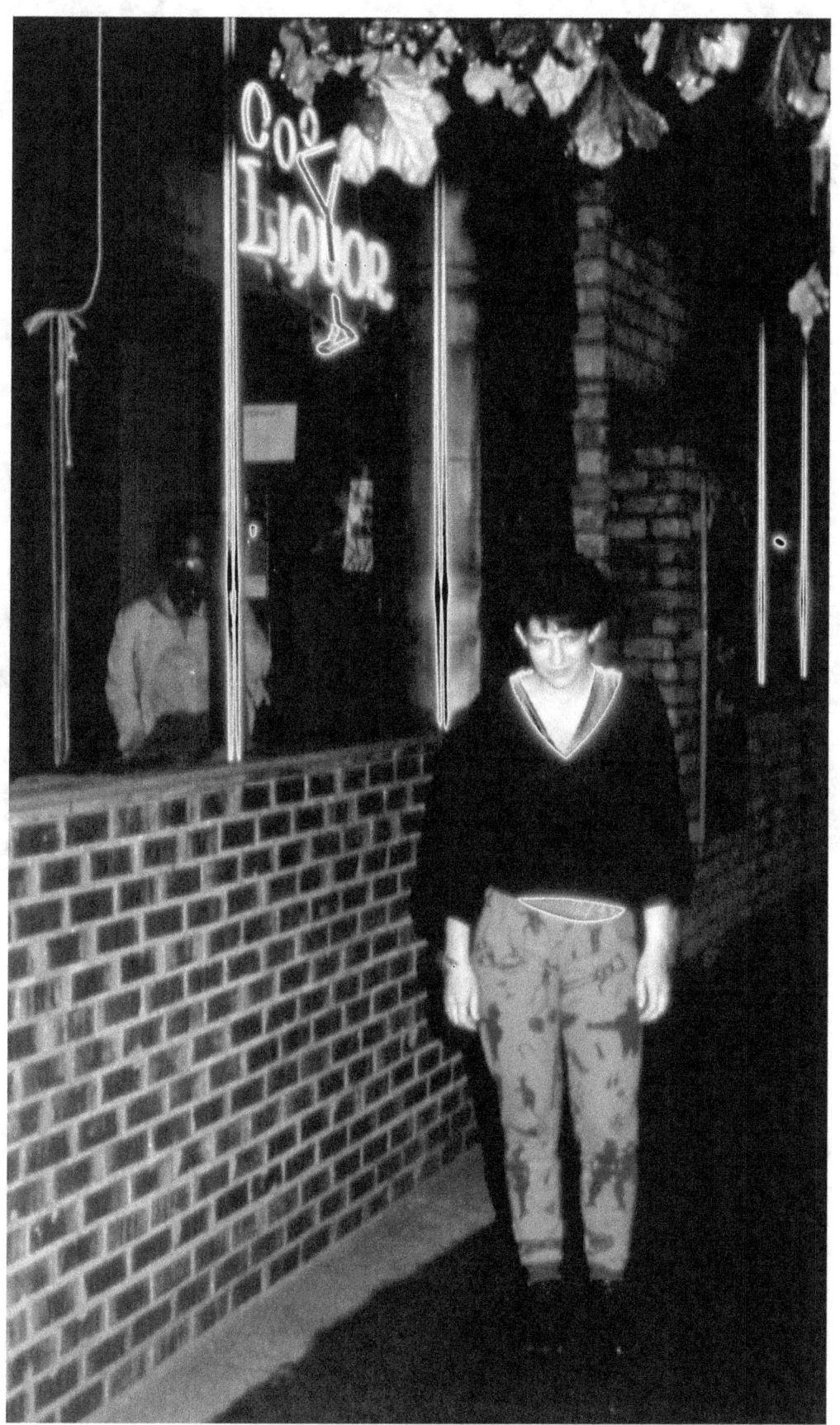

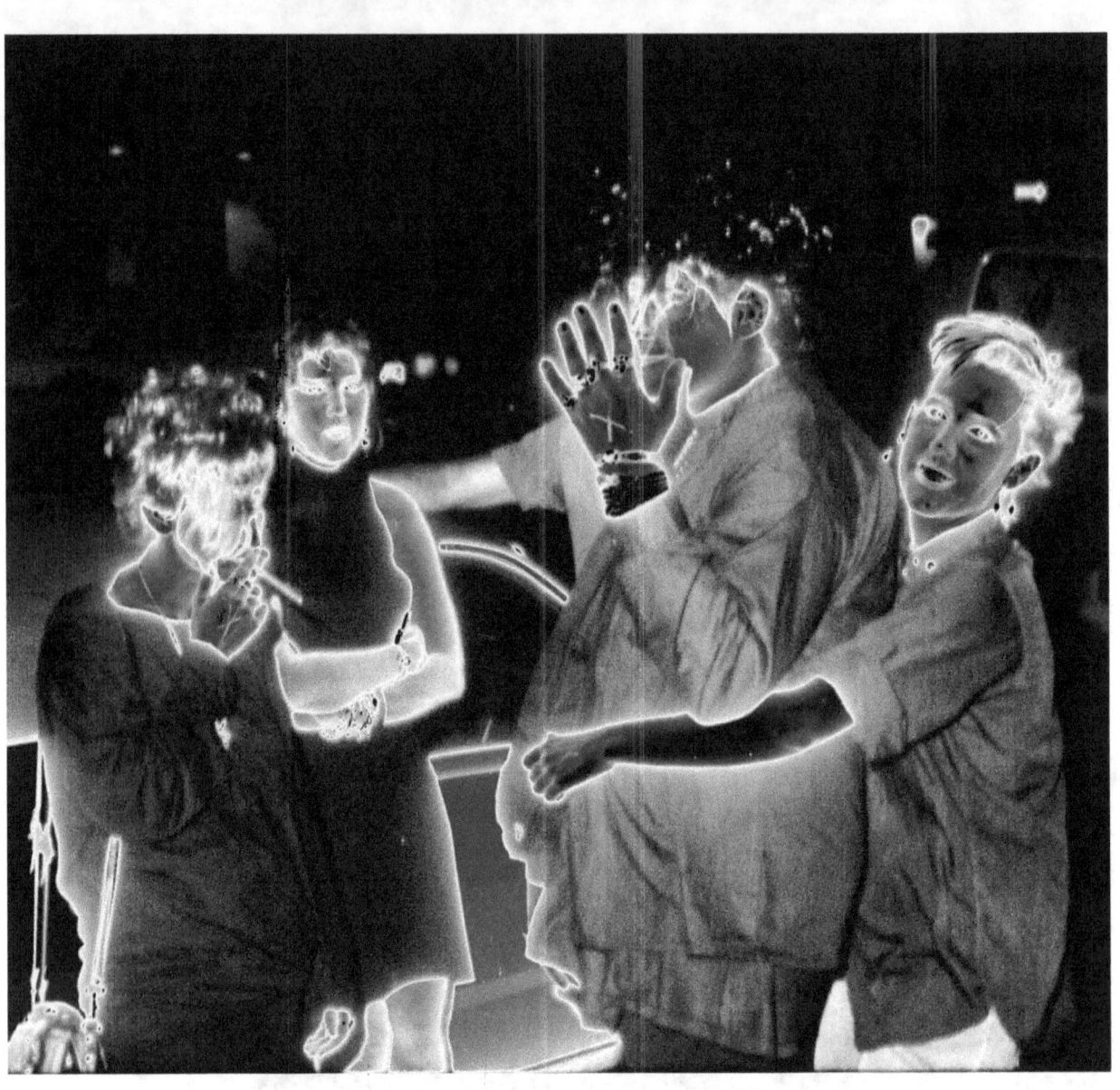

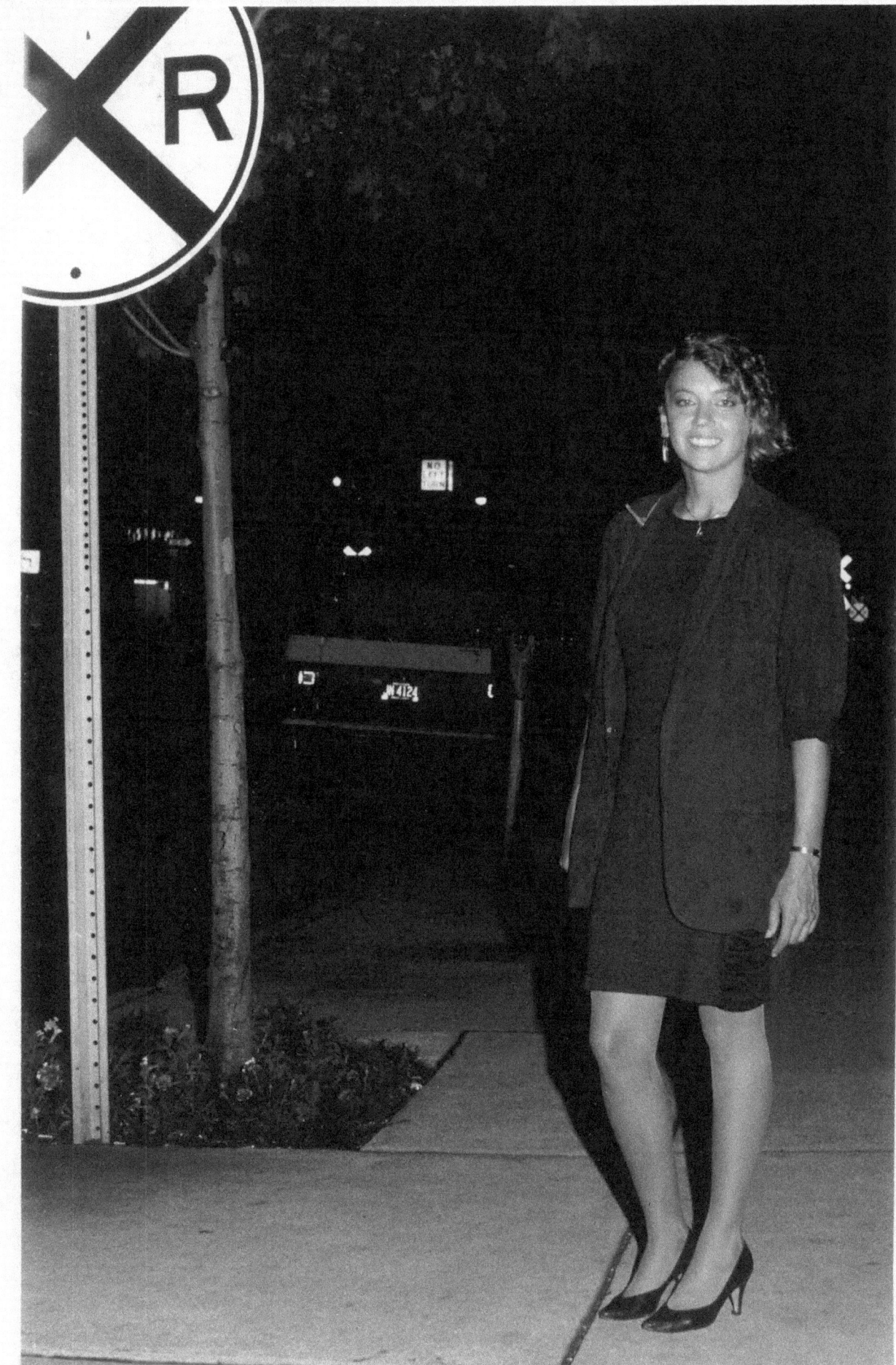

Now you know this is going up all over town.

Do I have to sign my life away here? Like if I get famous your going to show this?
I am going to be famous you know.

Looks like gang warfare.

What you got pulled over for drunk driving? "No I got pulled over the first night I bought Steve's car." you bought Steve's car? "Yeah I was just rock & rolling down Howard and I had just learned to drive a stick. So I was concentrating on how to drive a stick and it was all lit so I didn't have my lights on. I didn't even think about it because it's all lit and they pulled me over for not having my lights on. Well I couldn't tell. It's just like daylight driving down Howard at night!"

Now were'd you see me? And what did I say to you? What am I doing here really? See now you know how I felt, it was like "oh shit what kind of trouble am I in?"

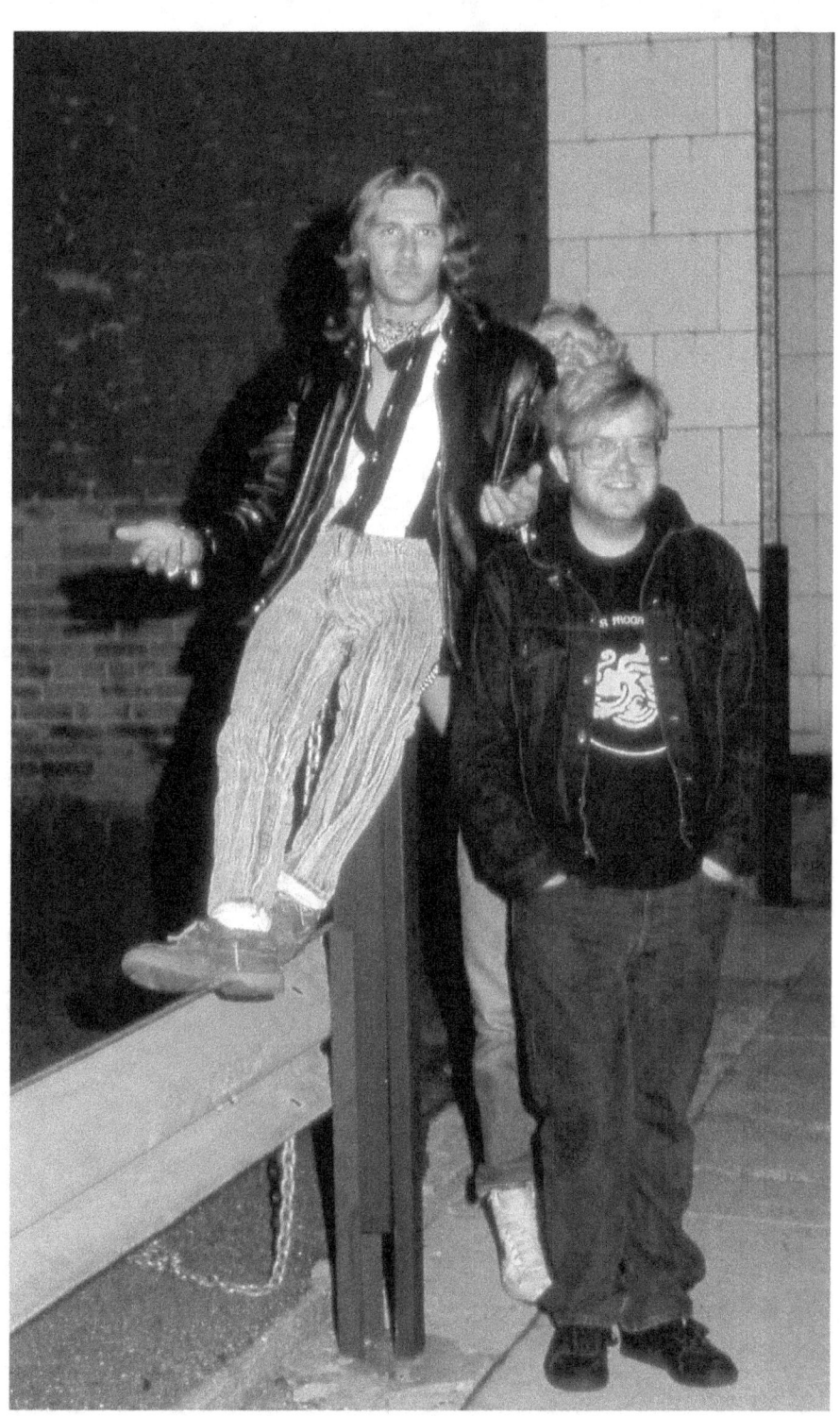

Well I'm having a bunch done Friday, I guess we'll have it done.

We'll do it!

Okay, well wait a second.

How fun, oh you are fun, you are so fun!

Thats my address but we're not going to pass that along.

Oh of course I don't want to read it, I'm just going to sign it. I don't care, oh parent or guardian? I'll be your parent and you can be mine.

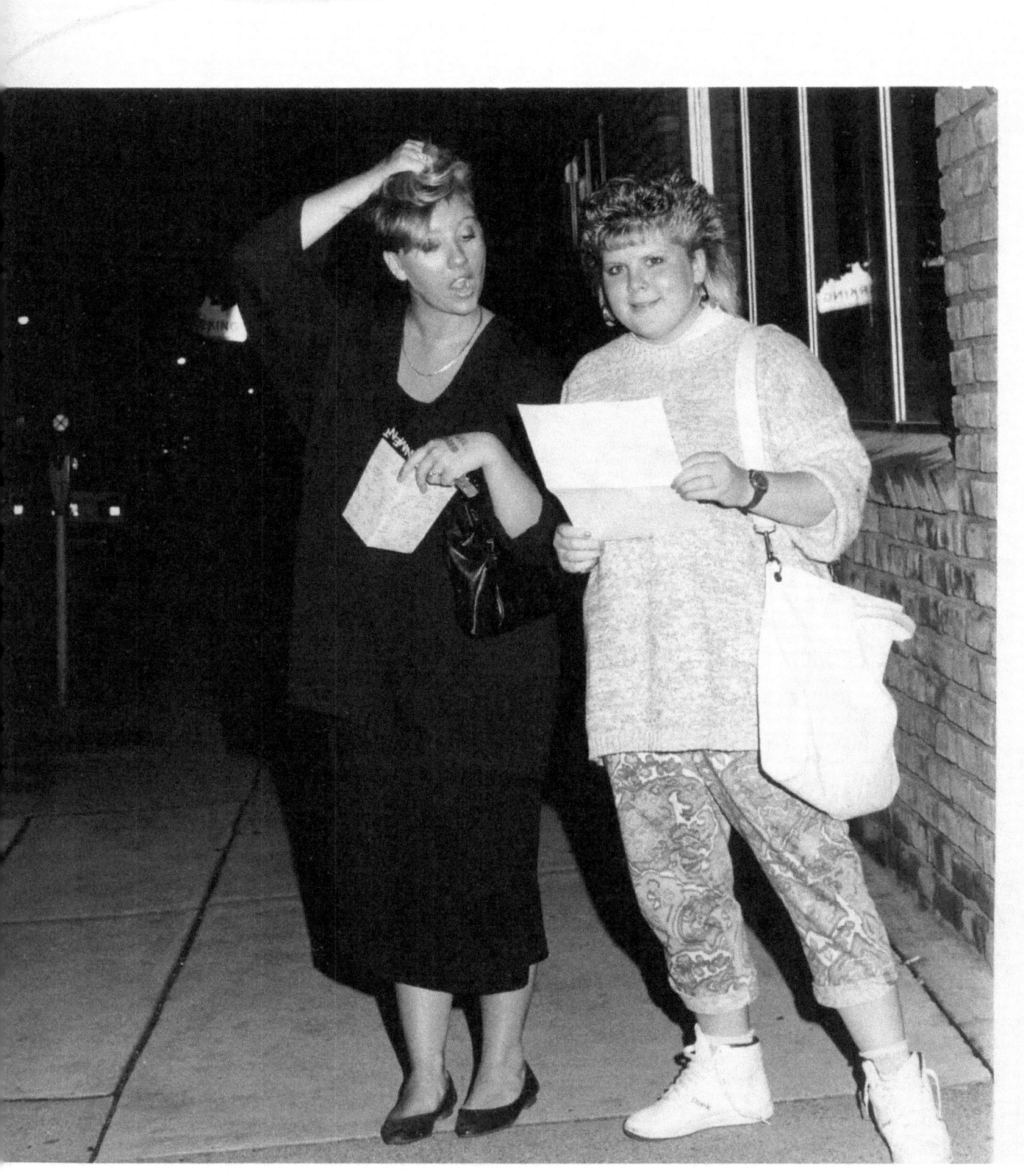

Okay I love to have my picture taken. Where do you want me to sit? Hurry I want it right away, we're gonna go get high and go back in there though.

I'm so stoned, oh you packed a full one.
-No I didn't it's only part way.
Here's my new Colibri lighter from Jacobsons.

We got here about 11:30 and we'd already stopped by my apartment and my friends apartment and we got here and I go, my purse is gone. We went back to my apartment and my purse was laying right in the middle of the street! Everythings in it, money, I didn't check the money. I'm sure the money's in it.

My drug friend is at home sleeping. He's such a drug fiend he's like " hey got any downers? got any pain killers?". I had unlimited prescription to percodan,. I was on it for a year, I was addicted to that shit. I was taking three to five a day. I had to go to the hospital because I hurt like this part of my knee and they kept giving me demerol. Demerol is just like thee drug have you been shot with demerol? Have you ever done a quaalude? The real ones? the capsules? I got into those big time, those are great you just lay back and go whoa.

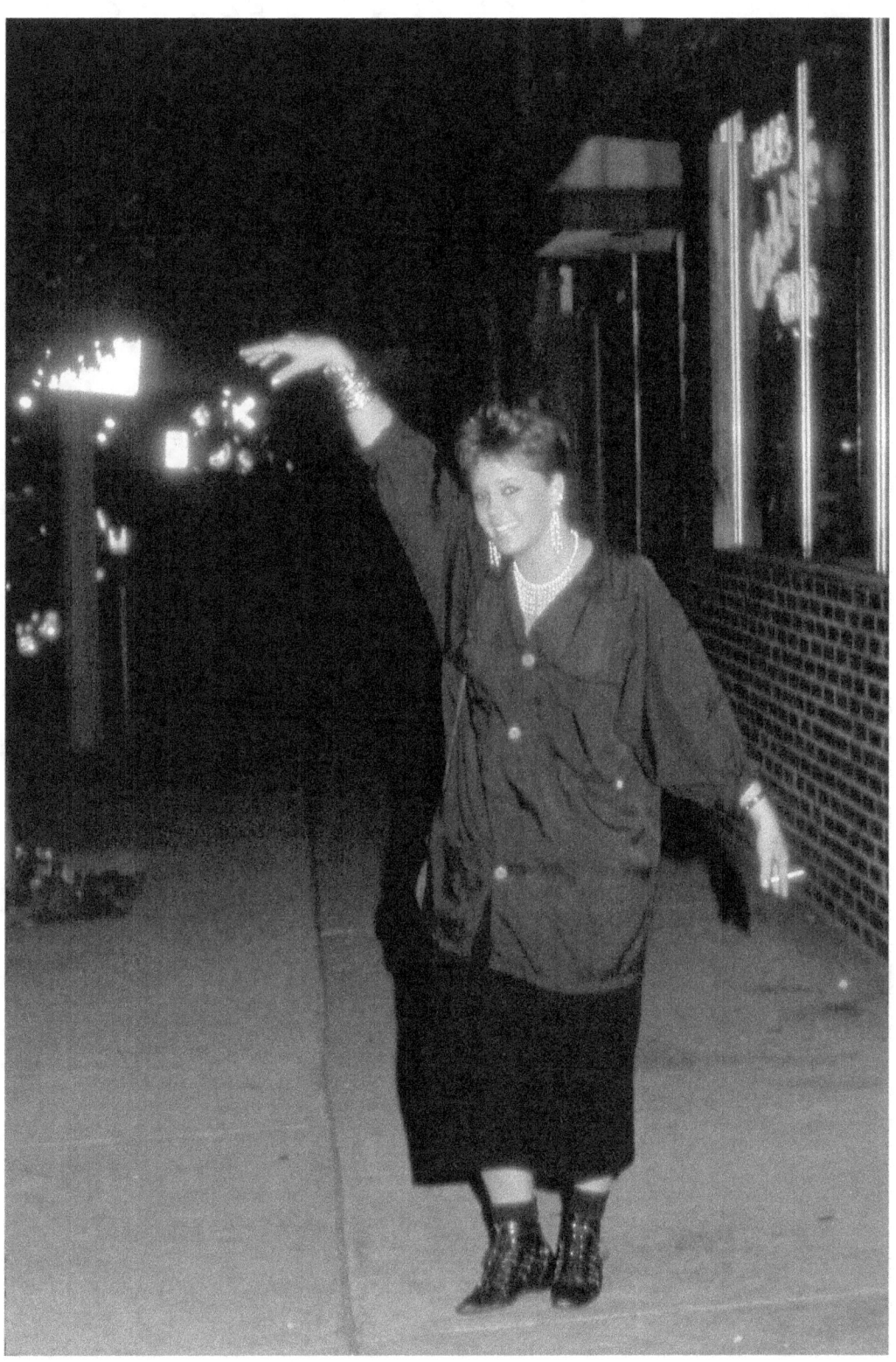

You should come in and get pictures of the band.
You could make some bucks that way.
—make me very famous!

Did you think we were going to be here? Don't park behind us asshole, we'll hit you real quick. I'd love hitting him, beat it man keep on driving honkey.

They freaked out when I walked in the door.
I haven't been in this city in like three months.
I knocked on the door and she say's "come in" and I walked around the kitchen corner and she's like oh shit!

I love photography because, man you can capture so many different moods with it you know.
And you can do so many different things. Painting is nice I love painting and stuff, but photography you know, especially black and white.

I'm just going to go home and veg out, I don't got class tomorrow.

Advertisings a great field you know. Thing is if you can get in New York and get into ad agency's there. Because I'm a marketing student and I kind of groove on advertising.

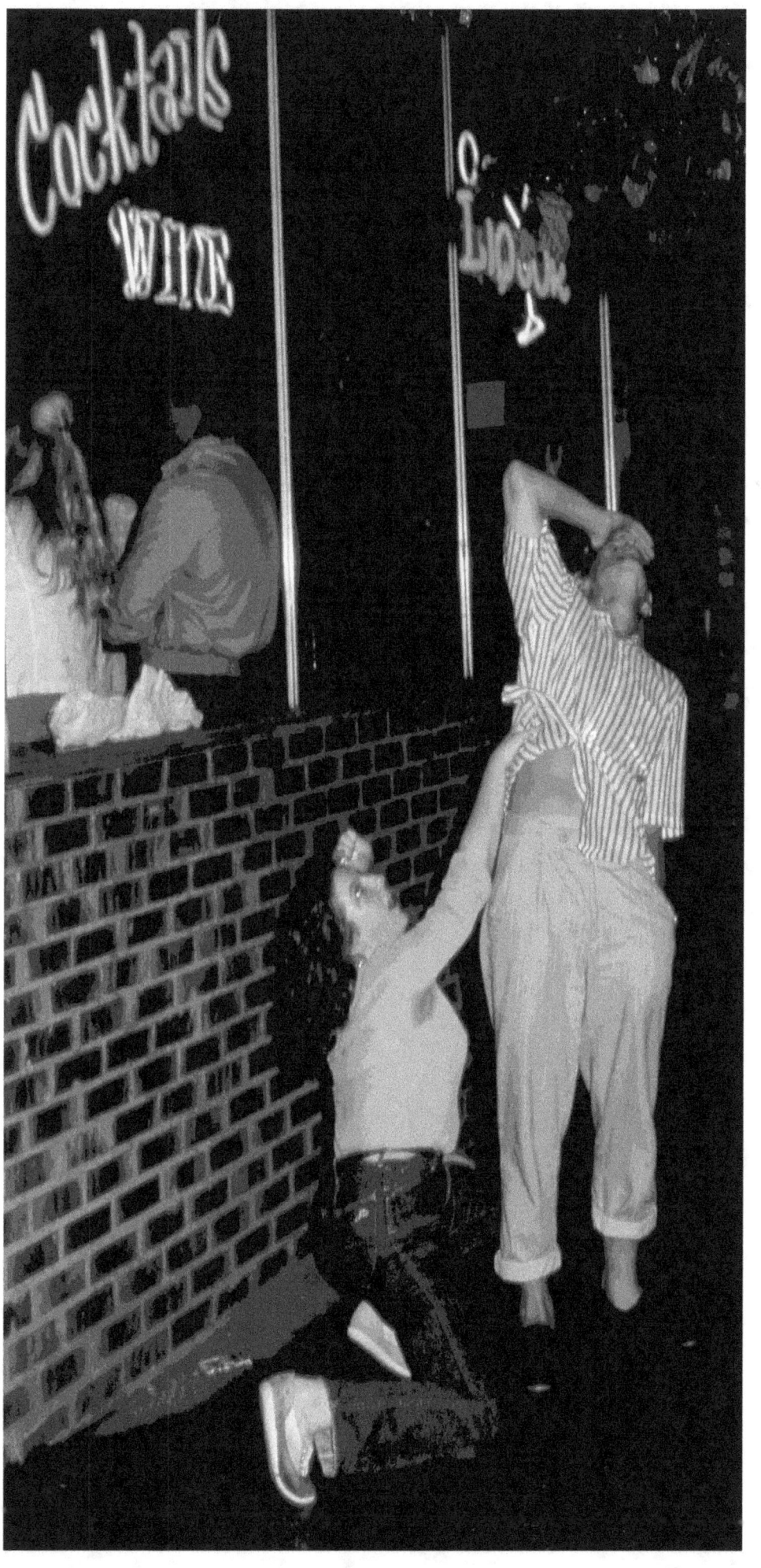

I'd like to go down south, go to Texas and see I've got some buddies down there I haven't seen in years.

Freaky thing happened to me today man, I was swimming and we where drinking, having a good time. And I see this guy walked in and I have not seen this guy since I was in eigth grade from Detroit area and I go _____ ____ and he looked at me and I swear to god and he knew me and he say's _____ ____ and I go nooooo! And we sit there and bullshit a while. He's a teacher, it was really neat.

You know what man,
their making it safe around here.

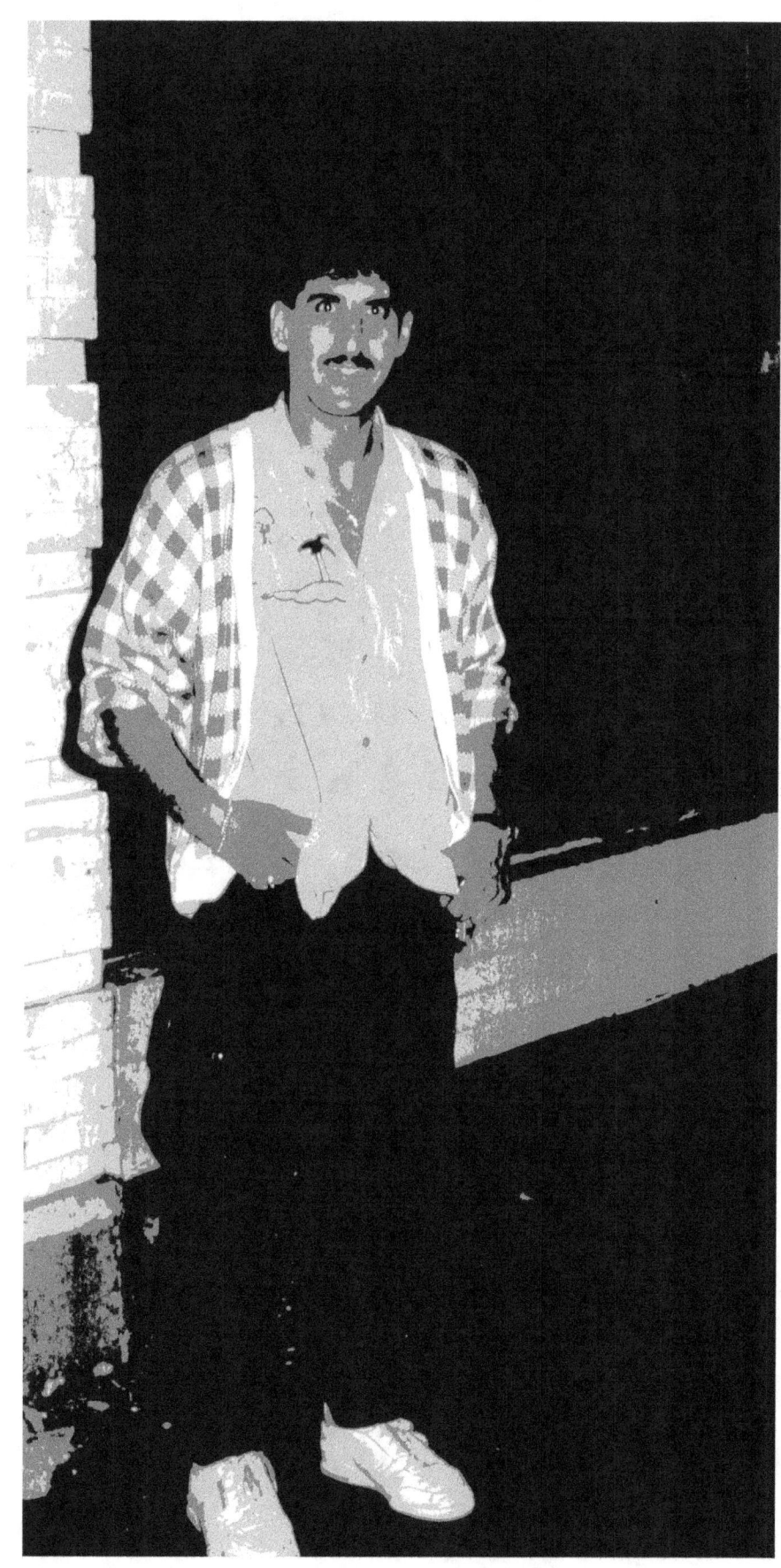

Pardon me, do we have to pay anything?

Alright take a picture of me.

You could take a picture of us together that'd be super cool.

Bowie, you call that music?
-I think so.
Is that what they call it?
-I like Dave I saw him in Vancouver about three years ago.

Well I went to amnesty international so there!
-Wow that outdates me.

That's cool man, I take pictures as a hobby.